AND OTHER VOYAGES

To Betty, Stephen, Tony, and Virgil

AND OTHER VOYAGES

Robin Magowan

MHO & MHO WORKS   1986   SAN DIEGO, CALIFORNIA

Parts of this book first appeared, in altered form, in the *Chicago Review, Descant, Exquisite Corpse, Hudson Review,* and *Shenandoah.* The chapter enqtitled "Persian Notes" was first published as a separate tract by Futharc in 1972.

1 2 3 4 5 6 7 8 9 10 J Q K A

For a complete catalog of other books being offered by Mho & Mho Works send a stamped, self-addressed envelope to:

Mho & Mho Works
Post Office Box 33135
San Diego, California 92103

Library of Congress Cataloging in Publication Data

Magowan, Robin
    And other voyages

1. Magowan, Robin—Journeys. 2. Authors, English—
20th century—Journeys. 3. Voyages and travels.
I. Title.
PR6063.A329Z463   1986   910.4   86-2535
ISBN: 0-917320-25-5

CONTENTS

INTRODUCTION

T RAVEL CAN BE DISCOURAGING, ALL
that dispersal of energy in the tedium and petty
harassments of what is, after all, an extraneous
culture. To combat it, it helps if you can think of yourself
as looking for something, a key with which to unlock the
treasure of your own buried imagination.

In the case of a civilization as ancient as Iran's, the
chasseur au bonheur has a near plethora of choice. Keys are
everywhere, a bit rusty, but still capable of unlocking a
door to a very rich survival. My relatives saw my trip as a
hunt for a Magic Carpet—surely somewhere in those
teeming bazaars there must be one capable of filling up
the hole in my living room floor?

Though I was hardly loath to spending a certain
portion of a Persian day watching layer upon layer of
celestial color being unrolled, it was something else I
wanted to experience—paradise! Here below that might
seem a bit much. But knowing that "paradise" derives
from the Old Avestan word for a walled garden, I decided
to hunt out gardens as an emblem of the larger poetry I
desired.

A good choice, not least because it took me away
from the mosques and the religious fanaticism that was to
come to a boil politically under Khomeini. If the gardens
proved almost as fictive as everything else in this now-
you-see-it, now-you-don't desert mirage kingdom, that,
too, might be a plus for the imagination.

Iran might have exerted a more profound
influence had I not sandwiched my six weeks there around
another trip to Greece. Looking back, it is tempting to
claim that I was torn between the two. Yet while I revel-
led in the sensation-crammed, hold-your-breath-and-dive
pools of Persian life, the country for all its poetry
remained unavoidably opaque, not to say Asian. Whereas
Greece seemed direct, composed in James Merrill's mar-

velous line of nothing but . . . "Essentials: salt, wine, olive, the light, the scream."

In this Cycladic island landscape I walked, marveling at the rocks, the fig trees, the flower-splattered fields; the odd temple column that existed not so much to make a site of worship as for the perspectives that the patterns of light and shadow brought into play: the dark blues of the water, the distant blobs of white building, so like another hillside's unmelted snow. Where had the labor for these isolated houses, chapels, come from? Or was there a race of masons ceaselessly pouring forth these molds of curved, perfect white?

So on the island of Astypaleia I envisaged a pair of cities forming: one white and high like the prow of a ship pointing out above a hillside's rubble, the other a port of pinks, ochres, browns. No wonder the child playing at blocks in me melted before all these curves within curves of dome and arching street, each so small and refreshingly cool if you only had the feet to poke along their basil-scented passageways above a sparkling sea; a whole civilization stuck, if not in the sky, then in the next best place, the lip of a volcano. For whole mornings in that spring of 1962 I walked, absorbed by the vaulted architecture, the white lines with spots of vertigo dripping onto a harsh incandescent blue.

I remember an Easter walk on Paros. Across the bay, beyond where the sea, a giant crab, pincered in, mountains rose, seemingly immense beneath their morning crust of shadow. Higher, having ascended through the port city's labyrinth of coiling, chalk-white streets, cradles to the mouthing wind, the valley road spun, high like a waist, its way threaded through transparencies of sea-whitened olives. Fields rippled out in tiers of green and gold speckled with poppies—as many poppies as green stalks of wheat—with maybe in a corner the white cube of a farmhouse, absolutely modest, yet with its whitewash binding fields and sea in the same flowing salve of sky.

Ahead the road glimmered like a sword as the eye sheered downwards, past little blue-domed houses, all terrace (with steps like lumps of sugar), to where in a pot of flame, the sea funnelled the last oils of day. What amazed was the legato joining of the whitewash, the cobbles reaching down and like a tongue drawing up the warmth from a source several bays away. How sensible in a fuelless island! And suddenly I understood the power of an Orphic flute. On an island where the light is like a note of song even the rocks can be seen to dance.

One evening I went with friends out beyond Piraeus to a roadside strip in Perama where the navy sailors came to dance and flirt with the male prostitutes. The cafe we found ourselves in was very plain—some four or five tables and a jukebox. The only food served was chicken and, if you wanted it, watermelon. Since the sailors were poor—the average navy wage was four dollars a month—it was not inappropriate to offer one or another table a round of beer. Now and then in response to a song some tall, cucumber-shouldered youth would stand up and, fingers clicking like a priest in a dream of stones, sketch out his dance.

Perhaps after a few steps a friend would join him, holding out his handkerchief. Around him the dream would turn, dispensing out of thin white trousers quietude, elation, manna. Onward the two would move, circling as on the rim of a glass, their hands fat, soft-spinning flowers, their feet spokes in a cycle of prayers. Both seemed very happy, sensing through the jukebox's din the hands of all of us around them, breaking in green time like plates.

I did not know then that these Turkish and hashish influenced *rebetika* I was watching were the dance music of the Greek navy (just as the *tsamiko* with its dives and heavy, serpent-like music is that of the army); or that the sailors themselves regarded Perama as their great *scuola di ballo*, comparable to what Wimbledon might be to a tennis player. But I couldn't help but be affected by what I had seen and in the back of the taxicab on the way home found myself jotting down the germs of what was to become my first real poem.

While in New York two years later I called upon Aristodomos Kaldis, a Turkish-born Greek American whose little painting in a friend's home of a pair of donkey ears peeping out of some long grassblades had been my first indication of what Greece looked like.

Somewhat naively I told Kaldis that I had saved up some money and was thinking of going to Greece for the summer. I added that my wife and I had been much taken with Paros, but for variety's sake wanted to try another island where she might be able to paint.

Kaldis would not hear of the bare, architectureless Cyclades. A painter, he said, needed "verdura," and he proceeded to extoll the virtues of his native Lesbos with its ninety-two villages, its famous bays and thousands of olive groves. When I asked where we should stay he suggested Mythymna, a fishing village across from the Dardanelles on the northeast tip with an art school where he had taught in years past. It was here, he said, that the dolphin rider, Arion, had swum ashore, bringing to Greece his Asiatic meters. A village away down the coast was Petra, thought to be where Achilles had retired in a huff after Agamemnon had forced him to give up Briseis. In the other direction, directly opposite Turkey, was the hamlet of Eressos from whose cliffs Sappho had leapt.

I knew of Mythymna as the setting of Longus's second century romance, *Daphnis and Chloe*. But more than these ancient associations it was the island's proximity to Turkey and the vanished Lydia of Seferis that drew me:

shores steeped in the perfume of nights
Among the singing of birds, waters that left on the hand
The memory of a great good fortune...[1]

It took a while, but I eventually found my dance, the zembeikiko, or struggle with the eagle, as the Turks know it. From then on nothing counted but this dark brooding rhythm and wherever it led me I went. On my sore feet, shaking, much of the time. But sometimes, too, on horseback, followed by this shepherd, George, in polished riding boots and deep gray, aristocratic-looking hair.

This may not be the place to defend the pleasures of anonymous sex. But just as birds and wildflowers require special lenses, so with an African one has to get up close enough to run a hand over the purposely placed circumcision scars, or reflect on the earrings, those tiny red globes that the prostitute entrusts with a smile. Exoticism, when mutual, can be a license to discover: those crowded sensations pressing in where all swims and rains and dissolves; sealing me off and making me one with the street. It was this, maybe, I bore away. Not a picture to stick in my billfold. Not even a record of what poverty reduces some women to—making love to the likes of me. Perhaps nothing but a wry, "A night, these trousers, just alone," when back home I found myself in the arms of a new lady. Where the mirrors of another, no less strange sexuality opened and into their dark, compelling mists I swam.

I had long admired the Tibetans, the spiritual strong men of Asia. Their culture had been blitzed by Mao's Chinese, but I figured much of its spirit could still

[1] "Argonautica," translation Rex Warner

be glimpsed in Sherpa Nepal. I was set to leave in March, 1973, for Katmandu when, one evening over dinner, my doctor—he of the first successful American Everest expedition—announced that he would be leading a month-long trek there in April, along the Rowaling and over 18,800 foot Tesi Lapcha Pass to the Sherpa high-lands. Would I consider going on ahead as planned to Katmandu and there joining up?

The doctor assured me that the trek was to be a walk, not a climb. The main thing was that we give ourselves enough time to acclimatize before attempting the pass. All I would need was a good, broken-in pair of boots, knee gaiters, and high altitude goggles. The trek would be catered with porters to carry whatever I brought, so long as the duffel bag did not exceed sixty pounds. Whatever reservations I might have harbored about group expeditions, here was an opportunity to learn to live on my feet, binoculars in hand, among the flower-ing rhododendrons.

Though I could not have anticipated it, the climb over Tesi Lapcha was to mark a final emergence: into something that could almost be called, because of the attendant pain, clarity. It's not for the views or flowers that you climb. There is something out there larger and, to survive, you must realign yourself. From now on only one thing counted, not spoiling the truth of those mountains.

AND OTHER VOYAGES

"Niemand wandelt unbestrafft unter Palmen."

— *Goethe*

"Seigneur innommable du monde, donne-moi l'Autre! Le Div...non, le Divers. Car le Divin n'est qu'un jeu d'homme."

— *Ségalen*

"The most urgently needed science is one that will show us how to make civilizations.*"*

— *Michaux*

PERSIAN NOTES

CERTAIN COUNTRIES, NO MATTER how frequently visited, seem unreal. Such was America before de Tocqueville and such is Persia today—the Persia of Chardin and Montesquieu that now goes by the name of Iran. What these countries have in common (besides remoteness) is their vagueness, one that ends by confounding all who would write about them. What is one to say about a country mostly desert and mountain range, where there are few people, no women (none with faces unveiled), and where to travel at all requires that one possess both a dust mask and spare intestine.

In the face of such hazards the traveler does what he can. He visits the principal cities, all quite modern—their predecessors have been razed—and the important monuments, of which there are maybe five or six. He may even find a friend who has a car, and with his help, something of the old Persia, the Persia of the Alhambra, of travel books and museums, will come through: a mosque here, its blue dome encircled by wind; a garden with battered mud walls and a pergola where he can walk with no one following, pointing at him. And there are trees, two or three maples. And water, just the sound (water that is seen distracts, especially water with goldfish or lilies in it). And flowers that don't spell anything. For a moment, he is happy. Something has gotten through, a stray scent that the time vacuum of the desert plateau has miraculously embalmed.

With the sense of an intuition confirmed, he goes home, satisfied, until some friend points out that, really, couldn't he have seen more of the essential Persia by spending an extra hour or two at the local museum, the one that had first given him the notion of going to this far-off country which, in his simplicity, he has credited with the invention of paradise. So, at any rate, he had thought of it; a people so enamoured of beauty as to be utterly helpless before anything possessing it—a horse or a twelve-year-old boy. To oblige his friend he goes to the museum. Together they stand in front of the case of 12th century lustreware. There are many pots hopelessly jammed one against the next, most of fine quality. Then he sees it, a pot with a blue, almost violet ground intense as the Persian sky itself. On it someone has painted a face round and smiling, a face like a bell whose black curves move outwards against the rim until they seem entirely to fill it—like a peach tree seen at the end of a long geranium-studded pool. It stands there in its arch, humble, its white blossoms perfectly still, like a friend who comes and with his smile completes your happiness.

□

Beauty is momentary in the mind. Nowhere is this more true than Persia, where it is so frequently the *idea* of something that is impressive—the way, say, a garden is laid out rather than anything realized in bald mud pathways and cypresses. The traveler who comes looking for a garden (it will have been marked on the tourist map issued by the local municipality) may find nothing there, the whole thing having dried up like the famous river outside Shiraz. Like oil, a garden is something not so much to be seen as divined, an invitation of leaves extending over high mud walls.

Looking for a garden you enlist on a tour which promises to take you through the whole of the city (if its main street is the Four Gardens, there must be one or two still somewhere?) Well, you are wrong, there is nothing, only a pair of silly shaking minarets giving onto distant grape-colored mosques, and some storks nesting amid the domes of a nearby slum. But you have come too far to give up. Climbing back into the taxi, you mutter another name. Fifteen minutes later the chauffeur pulls up before what seems the usual assembly of mud and stones. While he waits, a wicker gate opens and you go in. The outside consists of a modest pergola strewn with vine leaves and unopened wisteria, under which a lone student, book in hand, walks, memorizing his required verses.

Soon, other spaces disclose themselves: banks of grass into which pansies have been sown with a richness that at first affronts and which one ends by accepting, as one accepts an old lady's jewels; little five-sided pools bordered by a screen of cypresses and set off in turn by bleak potless terraces where a volley of crows sits feasting, their color a jangle of gray and gold in the luminous March air.

The remainder presents a crazy-quilt of quince, plum, peach, cherry, pear, pistachio; delicate maidenly ashes rising white to a considerable height; then, all of a sudden, a hoop of green, like a skirt held high over the head; everywhere, the bright extravagance of the judas tree. All this is jumbled pell-mell to create a profusion of color, the sense of the whole natural world being there, contained—in a word, plenitude.

If the Persian wants shade, he constructs it. With a bit of not too acidulated soil he makes himself a bower, and there plants four or five maples so as to form a ring (or if he has the space, a long rectangle). This he laces in turn with the sound of water, water flowing in a perpetual conversation. Along the channels he strews banks of narcissi and fat-mouthed irises whose color is laughter, ebullience. If then he is able to induce a pair of nightingales to nest in some adjoining shrub his happiness knows no bounds. He sits there with maybe some tea before him set on a silver tray, and on a carpet, heaped-up bowls of oranges and black dates which he serves you himself, smiling, never having seen you before, and knowing no words that will do in place of a smile.

In a country of mainly desert where everything must be built of mud and smacks of impermanence, little survives that has not been willed. These gardens are thus things like friendship for which there is no necessity, and like friendship, only in the continued exercise of the will sustained. Perhaps tomorrow it won't be there, or something else—an earthquake or government confiscation—will have intervened. And the gardens, you feel, sense this. They would like nothing better than to turn themselves into carpets—the carpet that you mount to ride away into nothingness, much as the modern Persian steps into a car and heads out into what is for him a vast undulating lake all breath, stars, and the tinkle of shattering glass.

It is easy to understand how a traveler can come home from a six-week stay feeling he has been living in a continual mirage. From a contemporary point of view Persia is an impossible country—much as Russia must have been in the latter 19th century, or America prior to 1890. As countries they were bizarre abstractions, things one believed in if sufficiently enlightened; not places with real borders and a homogeneous national character. Anyone today meeting a Persian might have difficulty believing that this Iran of his was not some new nation created out of whim by Rand McNally. What keeps it united isn't anything more than a minority language—and, in the final analysis, a body of poetry. What is one to say of a country that exports carpets and caviar—along with oil—for foreign exchange; that boasts the most expensive hotels known to tourism; that votes parliamentary funds for an artificial lake outside Teheran so as to have water-skiing.

To get anything accomplished the Persian must hie himself abroad, and rarely is he enticed back to the daily life of intrigue, outright lies, and endless, endless cups of tea. One suspects that, without tea, no business would ever be transacted, nor would there be any official-dom left on its feet. Yet these annoyances that make travelling so frustrating enable the Persian in his private life to turn himself out like a carpet for a friend.

The Persian, unable to go abroad, surrounds himself—blank man that he is—in an onion skin of abstractions, differing one from the next as the typical Noah's Ark garden differs from the sexual squalor of the old-fashioned orange garden with its beds of marigold, its hornets and crows reposing upon their squares of rich gleaming mud. In him these abstractions melt into a music as chaotic as anything else in Persian life—without beginning, middle, or end because essentially without hope—a music that, as one becomes accustomed to it, takes on the colors of thought itself, and that initial pain to which Rilke ascribed the source of all true poetry.

Unable to believe in a prospective future, without even a verb tense to express such a notion (one doesn't say *I shall*, but a more tentative I wish to), he must sustain himself in a present as magically continuous as those end-less flower-studded meadows in which the Persian of the miniatures sits. As we see him there, face without outlines like a young child's, he is happy, sated, very near sleep. But unlike the Western counterpart who exists only in his anticipation, and must realize it all in his lunch break (how well one knows the scene afterwards, the frayed secretaries, the aspirin tablets), everything here, the courtiers sitting under a distant peach tree tuning their lutes, the girl whose head dandles in his lap like a ripe bough, promises that he will wake and wander forth, the paths opening before him: long vistas down which the hands move in a silence of years—of all that grows—while around him the sorrow-world of blossom falls, their notes distinct as crystals. Under the spell he has become that child drunk on his first legs for whom the sky's blue is hope. It is there, so near as it settles on its frame of bare, mustard-colored hills, that he feels he can reach up with his hands and greet it, mouth bursting in a great pod-like grin.

When these childlike abstractions succeed it is as miniature, private creations. To see them otherwise is to be deceived. For the traveler who insists on inhabiting a greater scale there is always Persepolis, a structure that dwarfs even those palaces of the Versailles type, built to be seen from a horse. First, the whole surrounding landscape looks outsized, made up of greenish-yellow hills that stretch away into the lowered sky like shaggy camels; sky and hills being so much of the same tone that it is impossible to tell where one leaves off and the other begins. Nearing it the haze thickens. The plain looks infinite. Then suddenly the palace bursts upon you, its great columns looming from their inflated platforms like the one and only palace in the one and only kingdom in existence.

The situation of this great palace at the top of this once extraordinarily fertile plain of Marvdasht is what impresses. Beside it the glossy repetitive friezes with their processions of tireless Medes and Persians trouping one after another up the same set of stairs, the portals on which the same inevitable lion, its facial muscles contorted, is seen gnawing the same donkey—all this may strike one as rather overdone. The gestures are so stylized that the spectator feels shut out, repelled, and if he allows himself to be so, humbled. The Persian, though, has gotten over this, and in a shrunken world has gone on to create a culture as fragile and as human as his sense of flowers.

Teheran

At the impossible hub of Persian life is Teheran. Essentially a Qajar creation it has grown from several thousand in the early 19th century to over two million. Of this early Teheran little survives, other than the bazaar, and the Khake Golistan with its famous peacock throne. The latter is a pastry-tiled chateau interiored with much cut glass, large golden cuckoo (or rather peacock) clocks inscribed, "This superb piece of machinery was made by Thomas Byrne near the King's palace, 50 St. James Street." To the bearded Qajar, Napoleon had contributed a set of frescoed Sèvres depicting his campaigns, the Czar a cheezy turquoise-set sword. One gathers what they must have thought of him. For the modern visitor the interest lies elsewhere: in the carpet-strewn floors; the relatively bare and gleaming garden with its rows of large tufted plane trees; the long lateral façades on which desultory repairs are being carried out under the eyes of a pair of bayonet-wielding guardsmen.

Following this, a taxi-ride back through the modern city may reveal little other than the horrors of neo-Parthian government architecture, and the usual well-suited or veiled Teherani going about his business. On curbstones, sunburnt men sit polishing oranges with pink nylon toothbrushes. Occasionally the traffic is punctured by a tall gaunt man with the typical Pahlavi cap on his shaven crown, pushing a silly blue cart (equally tall and narrow with tiny wheels) filled with pots of long red and white carnations whose stems wave back and forth as he maneuvers between the stopped cars. Along a deep gutter women squat happily, sipping water and washing their hands. Men in overalls and yellow caps sleep face-down on a patch of sunlit rotary, oblivious to the traffic and the figure in white handkerchief-wrapped head and red shirt streaking past on a purple bicycle.

The traffic is of a virulence that even by Los Angeles standards seems appalling. Not a car that isn't in some way damaged: a fender, a scratched door, a dented hood.

One can sympathize with the recent premier who had an import tariff levied on them as a luxury his country could not afford. Since to the Teherani the car is a means of attaining paradise, the tax proved unrealistic, and the premier was himself dismissed. The legislature, wiser, has set aside each year a considerable part of the oil revenue for highway construction. But the Persian, with an instinct for self-preservation that has served him well against his numerous conquerors, has seen to it that few of these projects pass beyond an initial surfacing. Funds are diverted, and every few months a number of the cabinet is to be seen at Mehrabad Airport, on their way to join their colleagues in Zurich and Long Beach. In Teheran few car-owners do their own driving. Instead they hire a chauffeur newly arrived from the country, much as a hundred years ago a man drafted would hire a peasant to take his place in the army. This chauffeur (since paradise is at stake) in turn hires someone with a suit and dark pointed shoes and maybe a flower in his left ear to sit by him in the front seat, ready whenever they hit something to leap out and gesticulate.

With all these chauffeurs and their boyfriends and the workers hired for nonexistent construction projects, Teheran's population has more than doubled since the war. Fortunately the city's declivities have permitted the Teherani to construct his one-story houses in overlapping mud tiers, without the high rise's visual affront. For the more well-to-do there is modern architecture to which the Persian has added his particular refinements. Thus his houses have no windows, or a mere slit such as one finds in medieval towers, through which the day's weather (dust, snow) may be reckoned. And his gardens are all of the compound variety. If asked why, one is told, "Thieves." Against a creature whose resourcefulness rivals Zeus's no precautions can ever be too elaborate.

If this spectre of endless rectangular brick is dismal enough, what of the *chador*, the wall which encloses every woman from nose to toe. Unlike such vaguely similar equipment as the raincoat or mumu, the *chador* is primarily a wall for the face. If you blunder upon a naked lady taking a courtyard bath her first instinct is to grab a towel and wrap it around her face. She will then stand carrying on the usual exchange of amenities until a servant arrives. On a busy street it is not uncommon to see a woman with a baby under each arm, holding the veil between clenched teeth. A habit held onto this firmly is not easily shaken, no matter how many royal edicts are issued. In Teheran there are a number of emancipated women who don't wear the *chador*. But not one would think of going out without first covering her face in a half-inch-thick glaze of red powder, in every way just as effective. Like most walls the *chador* is not altogether unshakeable. It can be adjusted to suit the needs of a moment, much as a Western lady with attractive legs will fidget with her skirt—to call attention to what lies under it.

The Provincial City — Gardens

At the end of a body of sand the provincial city appears. First, the waterfront of trees strung in an explosion of tall greens around the city, giving it the illusion of a garden. Next a bridge, its brick spanning what may be no more than a bed of stones and a parked solitary jeep. Then the inner city with its rows of little rectangular mud-baked dwellings and criss-crossing powder-white streets winding on and on in an endless maze, like those tunnelled castles children construct to roll their marbles through: a jigsaw puzzle of holes and sudden luminous spaces out over which the blue of a mosque dome plays, much as fountains play in an Italian city.

To the man of the desert the city is paradise—*that place where things grow.* Since rain isn't all that common (in Shiraz, *the* garden city, it hadn't rained in three years), this matter of growth may be illusory. Yet it is one that the Persian believes in, and in acting upon it he transforms the city into a place where both he and his dreams can thrive. Thus any revenue the governor general's family does not need will go into tree planting and flower-clock rotaries. Shops have baskets of flowers calling attention to them, and the articles are displayed as if they were flowers. If by an act of grace a garden does exist—privately owned and so remote as to be practically unvisitable—it becomes a source of civic pride. Newspapers follow it with an avidity elsewhere reserved for the local ballteam. Such a garden need be no bigger than a rotary. In Yezd, outside the East Gate, there is one such rotary, containing an enormous statue of Shah Reza. At sundown half the town is there, come to observe the flowers as one might the skaters in Rockefeller Center, while around them traffic swirls and the near mountains glow.

If the city is gardenless the Persian does not let that faze him. He bides his time knowing that soon a holiday will leave him and his friends free to go forth (the women in the rear, bearing quilts and hand stoves) to one of the perimeter plantations where a shrivelled stream, told by the two or three scraggly willows of an otherwise treeless landscape, is all that remains of the great river Sa'adi once picnicked by.

In cities less fortunate an office staff will hire a car. And they swarm in, four and five to a seat, perched on each other's lap, on your knees, even in that space between the driver's left knee and the door. And they think nothing of driving forty miles to get to a place with nothing but a brick wall, an L-shaped outhouse, and maybe one tiny apricot tree, in whose shade the whole party will sit, playing bingo with the green fruit.

In this city spectrum the *ne plus ultra* is the garden that will be just water itself—white flowerless splashing roar. In Teheran to the north there are several such where at noon men come to dine like Huck Finns on wooden rafts that have been riveted in mid-torrent. The diner arrives, parks his car, and, hopping ibex-like, clambers from stone to stone up through a fantastic waterfall of maple and willow trees, pink knobbly mountains out of some miniature, while below in the rushing water men in blue pants and marigold shirts, coats off and heads in each others' laps, sit on carpeted rafts among mounds of watermelon, orange pop, and fried chicken. As you pass over them on the little wooden footbridges diners reach up at you with handfuls of pistachios. Upstream you spot other walking picnickers, swaying under carpets and melons. The walking is impossible—stones, slippery logs— but you realize that you can't fall, that the obstacles form only an illusion of peril, like a tunnel in a funhouse.

Later, you join the diners on their rafts. Here the dazzle is that of shirt whites set against eyebrows and blue-black hair; against the turquoise of a distant bridge railing; against your own shoelessness dipping food-begrimed hands into the roaring water; while you sit like a huge leaf, or, more exactly, a crow floating between trees. With the image comes the realization that, for the diners, it's not a raft they are sitting in, but a treehouse; the sort into which the child like a rocket climbs in order to fire himself off into his own white annihilating space.

This wish for flight receives impetus from a locale where the hedges really are of mud; where the unrolling of a carpet, or the soft, underhanded gestures of masons tossing bricks, are at one with the bubble-domed houses.

upward thrust of the petitioner's hands; each projecting, honeycombed arch caught by the next band of unseen brick.

It is as if over our earth there were another level—wave. Then sky. But a sky, a tile, mixed with mud, with us. Patterns demonstrating how we can climb that flowering lattice of color, and soar. At the top night itself, the lost boundaries of algebra.

What keeps it from giddy platonism is the Persian's sense of his momentariness. Who would soar if he had to drift around all day like a vulture?

Color is the beanstalk, tying property down while adding speed. A bicycle is red or purple, lampposts yellow, traffic railings turquoise. You get into a taxicab to find yourself in a swirl of plastic flowers, dolls, and belly-dance photos, all set off against fake zebra fur seat-covers. The color evinces the city dweller's protest against the surrounding desert. If he didn't feel its horror, he wouldn't be there.

With so much color, spatial relations change, and a man strolling in a bazaar is soon numbed by the head-jerking zig-zags of the hanging pots, towels, scarves, vests, bed fabrics. Children are not pushed about in strollers, but carried high, propped on a brother's shoulder, at one with the phantasmagoria of household life. In a garden patio only grass and pansies grow out of the earth. Everything else is suspended, a stream of pedestalled or hanging pinks, blues, reds among which the eyes move as if bathed. And when the Persian hoses, it is never the ground but the air, the walls, standing there for hours until he has created his own private mist. He does this, he says, to cool off the house for sleeping. But when the time comes he goes to the roof.

Dining

The Persian eats with soup spoon and fork, using the latter also as a pusher. In restaurants these arrive in a large glass of (hopefully) boiling water. They are often sent back.

The napkins—bits of colored glider paper—repose in another glass. *Ab-dugh*, a carbonated yogurt drink, is also on the table. As one is shown to one's seat, mint leaves are brought. The Persian eats them squashed in a flap of bread, or, if thirsty, swallows them plain. With everything, salt. One mixes it with the yogurt and sprinkles it on the cherries.

After the final courses of fruit and jam comes tea, served in a tiny glass over a saucer. It is consumed with two or three large lumps of sugar (biggest for guests), the Persian holding the sugar between his teeth and using the tea as a chaser. Rather than wait, most drink out of the saucer, pouring the tea in bit by bit, sloshing it around and adding sugar as desired.

Others sit around smoking huge water pipes. Maybe a friend sits near for comfort. But he doesn't talk and neither do you. After awhile, dizzy, but pacified by the inward concentration, you get up—with that look of a turtle surfacing.

Then sleep. On an eight-inch-wide ledge of sidewalk you see them, prone, fists clenched. Or upright in a chair, arms fervently twined around an enormous cash register. Or squatting over their heels in air, a needle point, a scooped flicker of dust in the great existence. These chest-high, cracked, differently-levelled cement sidewalks are the Persian's version of a balcony, and you would no more think of walking on one than of walking on a dining room table.

Dress

The Persian one meets in a provincial city carries himself with the air of a man blessed. To be part of such a complicated existence is happiness itself. A uniform not only satisfies him, it leaves him dazed, able to do little more than stand before a hall mirror lost in quiet self-absorption. At any hour you may find the entire hotel staff napping on a great length of carpet. As soon as you pass they spring to their feet and begin combing themselves, brushing off each other's coats and trousers.

Sometimes you may wake to a scene of impromptu wrestling in the courtyard. A maid servant clad in what looks like pyjamas (actually the national working dress) has her grip pitted around a man's suited leg. His is around her waist. Both lurch back and forth to the accompaniment of playful screams and encouraging yells from the maitre d'.

Most of the time the little yard is deserted: bare except for a rectangular pool where linen is washed, and a few plane trees towering over the side wall, pale trunks gleaming against the violet-blue sky; a stillness broken now and then by the white veil of a maid crossing, a copper basin on her head.

This narcissism also holds on the ministerial level, or so it may seem to a Western eye. The suppliant who wants a service performed is shown into a little waiting room. There for some fifteen to twenty minutes he sits while his presence is announced and the minister makes himself ready. The last silver lock in place (you have a glimpse of the final touches as the secretary draws back the door), he receives you, a sweet ineffective smile playing over his lips, genuinely happy to be talking French (so successfully, his syllables practically purr!). You quickly understand the strains your request would impose on his little staff. But you do come away admiring his blue suit, batiste shirt, and flowing silk tie; and that air, so wonderfully maintained, of a large refined mouse.

Dress is important to the Persian and he carries it off with an éclat that would make an Italian's eyes water. From the sneakered, white-robed mullahs—always seen hugging a wall—to the man in a homemade suit of blue and gray stripes fitted with a tie of the same startling cloth; to the hotel clerks in their waistcoats, with the 1880 high-nipped waist and long horseshoe neck, a definite style is apparent. To this the Persian adds his exuberantly tortured crag-like nose over which eyebrows extend like a fierce rainbow. Like other great noses this can have a tendency to levity. Those, like truck drivers, needing to inspire fear, take care to flourish thick bushy moustaches: nothing to distract from the pool-like solemnity of the eyes. And it is these eyes, along with their dark suits and night-colored hair, that give the avenue Persians their look of fantastically elegant, sad crows.

The hair may vary from a style flat in the middle with the sides swept back in ram's horns, to a carefully combed crest, as expressive as the backs of a pair of hands as it flops in conversation.

In more traditional cities this art gives way to that of the turban: green, if the wearer is a descendant of Mohammed; otherwise yellow, white, or a sprightly plaid. Some especially formal ones remind you of soap-bubbles that would collapse if you blew hard. When all this appears on a wide tree-lined avenue at 5 p.m. the effect can be quite startling. Imagine a whole street reeking of attar of rose!

Women

The women are harder to judge. If at all like the little girls in the bazaars they may well be the most beautiful creatures in the world. The trouble is that those 'wild black eyes' go by in the space of a smile, with nothing to prove it's not another mirage. Those with faces are either tribeswomen, dark-skinned and dressed in gowns of rose and saffron with skirts fluffed by rows of multi-colored petticoats; or women who survive out of archaic convention—like the harem type, wondrously plump, invariably in the same brown skirt and green lisle sweater, whose crossing of the street each morning at ten was obviously one of the day's great events. Men lined the curb and, as she crossed slowly, deliberately, barely able to lift each foot, a hush would descend, and with it a kind of respect, as when one sees a swan trying to walk on dry land.

With their glossy hair, definite brows, and large eyes Persian children are beautiful. They dart about the bazaar, smile, look serious, and charm as a butterfly charms. If they are girls their presence becomes especially important: on their faces rides an otherwise invisible world.

On the bus between Yezd and Kerman we came upon one of the usual indeterminate age (between eight and eleven), with a high child's voice and yet the manner of a woman long admired. Her props, besides her little girl's printed frock and leggings, were a pair of tiny gold earrings and a mop of henna-tinged hair. To the men she was at once child, sister, and prospective mistress. They tussled with her, and held her on their laps while they teased her and fed her bits of chicken; all to the mixed discomfort and pleasure of her equally beautiful, but subdued (and veiled) mother. Forty years earlier a sultan seeing such a prize, would have clapped her into his harem and left her there to ripen.

City Life

City life is easy to misjudge. First, there are many places where a tourist is not welcome. If you do get in you have to proceed hurriedly, not lingering for fear the inevitable crowd will collect. If the life is there it is like a manuscript in a public case, its illuminated page (chosen how? out of what whim?) shining up at you from under its foot of glass. It is hard to remain objective when everyone insists on treating you as so much moving revenue.

No sooner has the taxi-cab departed than here is each mendicant presenting himself. He twitches, capers about on whatever limbs he has, and, if sufficiently inspired, may even compose a poem about you, chanted in a delicious high voice to the general merriment. So the traveler who wishes to see anything must stand holding his hourly auditions, now and then rewarding one of the more promising with a coin, who takes it without a smile, a bow even, regarding it matter-of-factly as his due, to be subjected to a cool scrutiny and if below expectations, on the spot returned.

What one does perceive is a complexity as abstract and untranslatable as Persian poetry, that onion skin of endlessly overlapping allusion and association. Pare this away and one will find nothing—the void of the ordinary desert existence. Thus the smallest of operations such as buying a dozen carnations, or getting a pair of shoes shined, takes on a complexity that makes the dentist with his sprays and drills look like a piker.

One would think that buying a few flowers might be something swiftly dispatched. No, the vendor must bring out his whole stock, the two of you pore through them until at the end of a quarter of an hour twelve mutually satisfactory stalks have been assembled. Each of these must be wrapped: first in a fern leaf, then in a strip of costly newspaper. The whole thing is tied together—you are offered your choice of ribbon and colored paper. You pay, another ceremony which involves his going out into the street, complicated in its way as a stock exchange transaction, bless one another, and leave. And, later, your friends agree that the flowers *are* beautiful.

These operations are kept from being time-consuming by the mutual involvement that the succession of gestures enforce. In the midst of having your shoes shined, a forty-minute operation; he takes off the shoes, removes the laces, places a piece of newspaper under each foot, then with a fruit knife begins to scrape away; this done, the first of three coats of wax is applied, the cobbler preceding each application by searing the wax in his little brazier, (like a baseball pitcher going to the resin bag), and he gets up and goes into his back room, opens a drawer to emerge after a minute, with a single cigarette that he offers with a grace and thoughtfulness that only the truly poor seem able to muster.

Some Institutions

One culmination of this life of mutual respect is the zurkhana. One finds it in a back street; with a bench set aside for spectators and a small hollowed-out pit where men dressed in red plaid loincloths (worn hitched in at the middle and billowing out over the buttocks in a series of folds) assemble in the evening to exercise. Presiding from a raised platform is the owner-trainer, a huge figure in blue tights and a white T-shirt. While they bend and touch, he accompanies them on his two drums and chants verses from the *Shahnameh* interspersed with ejaculations and prayers to Ali (imagine Americans working out to Walt Whitman!).

After a series of initial exercises each in turn will pick up a little javelin. Holding it at arm's length he begins to twirl, going faster and faster to the accelerating drums until the circles under him come apart and he has to be caught (after which he hops about on one foot at the edge of the ring while the next spins).

The final feat involves throwing a club the size of a man's leg. The performer must juggle it (with others, naturally). Then, when he has gained control, throw it up end over end so as to catch it behind his back. Few succeed, but what counts is that he has thrown it and not been brained; that he has enlarged his fund of courage.

□

Another great bulwark of Persian life is the *hammam* or Turkish bath. One understands what a bath is for—to get yourself clean. Still, there is such a thing as being congenitally unclean. After being turned down by three bathhouses—it is Friday—we find one willing to admit us. We pay, are given tickets, and are shown into a locker room whose red-carpeted sides are separated by a cement runway or 'street' stretching down the middle. Here you must stand until you have removed that street part of yourself, your shoes. Handing them to the attendant, you mount a carpeted platform, to be girt in the inevitable red plaid bathcloth. You are then led, taking care to avoid the runway, into a modern shower, and left there—with soap, hot water, and the door drawn. This shower is not for getting clean, something no one can do alone, unaided; but to get you used to the idea of water, magic that it is.

After some ten minutes of this, the bather, feeling a bit let down, may find himself wandering out into a room that looks like a huge fish tank: scummy algae-green walls; a floor of red mortar where cockroaches can be seen methodically plodding about; and high overhead, a round glass dome giving the tank-like quality. Here at the bottom of everything one takes up a praying position, arms tucked behind, head tilted forward. And the attendant, armed with a sort of brillo pad, goes to work: neck, back, and forearms first, and thence down over the body. Each time you are turned over, the towel must be readjusted so that he does not come in contact with your private parts. Rinsing is taken care of by a couple of shaven-haired kids carrying half-tires of steaming water which they hurl out at you, jai-alai style.

Once all the dirt has been scraped away, soap is applied. After a second blasting from the tire-carriers comes a hair shampoo, a process of some intricacy. The attendant places a soapstone at the bottom of a plastic bag. By dint of much rubbing and blowing he causes a certain quantity of suds to form, which is then applied to the hair. No effort is made to clean the actual scalp. The attendant simply hits down with the flat of his palm, as if beating a rug. When he is finished you are led back into the original locker room, taking care, of course, not to step on the runway—else the whole process must be repeated! Never will you have felt so clean.

No less special is the dervish convocation. Everyone must know a little about dervishes, those Christian Scientists of the East, men of the begging bowl and the silver axe, who in Persia are credited with all sorts of magical powers, from sword-swallowing to the ability to walk on water. Their strongholds are the Kurdish hill towns of the West. It is here the traveler must go if he wants to see them in something other than their usual roadside isolation.

The meeting place may be a plain white room decorated with Sufi scrawlings, and a second interior room where the seance takes place. As each enters he is handed a large mug of tea. If he is a stranger and has arrived early, he may find himself cradling his empty cup for the better part of an hour while the head dervish, a portly man dressed in the white flowing robes of a negro revivalist, holds forth on the pleasures of dervishdom.

Now from the inner room comes the first liquid 'Allah'. Spectators line one wall, the other three being taken up by de-turbaned dervishes, heads nodding to the accompaniment of a large pizza-shaped drum. After the preliminary incantations they rise and begin a rearing, plunging, forward and back two-step that will get more rapid as other drums join in. With each step forward the long hair is cracked forward across face and chest. As in Haiti, it is the combination of elements that bring on possession. But unlike there where it is entered individually and with the greatest reluctance, here it happens all at once, the climax occurring when, at a signal, the whole ring suddenly links hands and in blind fraternity goes under.

Holding two ends of crackling wire the head-dervish steps forward. He gives them to the first chanter who plants them between his teeth, then dances, every now and then uttering a little whimpering moan. Next come two light sockets. The man inserts his thumbs and somehow or other blows the house fuse. With a wonderful calmness the head-dervish manages to keep everyone from panicking. Candles are brought, and before long the lights are back, and here is the same man with his two inserted thumbs proudly dancing.

Next, Saint Sebastian! The two cheeks, cheek and gullet, or using a somewhat longer skewer, across one ribcage to the other. After each insertion an assistant steps forward and with a rough gesture pinches back the hole (to prevent scarring?) This is to be followed by the severed head trick, the man walking holding it at arm's length à la Bertrans de Born. Not wanting to see it perpetrated on a shaven-head boy we leave, realizing there is a part of this life that must forever resist one. Still one can't help but admire those who, by pure discipline, can make themselves into lightning rods to God.

□

In the midst of this medley of elaborately sustained illusion the mosque appears immensely real—the desert reincarnated within walls of tile. Severely abstract, with inner domes composed of strands of interlocking brickwork, it has a delicacy that makes Istanbul's pencil-and-inkset mosques look like railroad stations.

The center, the celebrated *eyvan*, is a bare gleaming void, a desert where for once there is water, maybe no more than a trough for the hands, but enough to give the promise of holiness. At the ends, like a distant enchantment, stand panels of blue tile, mirages hardly different from those of the Persian sky. As one approaches forms emerge: large floral scrolls threaded with white; a labyrinth of blues starred here and there with a bit of orange or green or scarlet so as to suggest a trellised garden. Hanging above in a blaze of tile is the great dome which, as the sun strikes, expands to become a white flowing river in which all earthly life is summoned up and, as it were, contained.

What keeps the design from disintegrating under its own luxuriance (as in Indian art) is the respect that the Moslem Persian has for the unity of creation. First place goes not to the swelling volume of the dome, but to the band of narrow gilt Kufic that proclaims it part of a natural order conceived in the imagination by a unique Creator.

Travel

The great mistake in Persian life is to want to do something. Why suffer disappointment? Before embarking on a trip the Persian consults everybody: family, Hafez, the various mendicants. All invariably counsel prudence.

The man who must go somewhere should go by himself, in his own car if possible. If dining out he should request a private room. To go in a taxi is to mix. Several taxis and he is no longer master of his own taste. He is a clown.

Those who want to be clowns of course can, and Persian life is full of them. One sees them squatting on their heels listening to a storyteller in a bazaar, or in attendance at belly dance or soccer match. But one no more joins them than one would join the line outside a public lavatory.

It stands to reason that the Persian should try to keep his country away from you. So, after a brisk tour of the latest hamburger stands, swimming pools, and iceboxes (rarely working, but big, prominent, glowing with family photographs), he whisks you into his Impala, and with you in there, safe from others, sets off for his paradises: rainy Caspian Sea beaches where his fellow Teherani sit with that look of shipwrecked Shakespearean actors.

He succeeds to such an extent that after three weeks of relentless driving you may well wonder what you have seen: a little girl waving as she holds her even smaller brother under a tree; shepherds in drab, double-breasted suits (one seen desultorily fanning a favorite ewe; then, exhausted, lying down alongside); turquoise sweatered—and leotarded—tribeswomen glimpsed in the rice fields against huts of conical thatch; others, pink pantalooned, or scarlet robed, giggling, probing one another, bouncing a melon on a hand. Only once anything special, at a source-fed lake reached after a teetering drive that included the fording of two rivers: of a milky depthless blue, warm only on the surface (not where the hand reaches in to stroke), with boys diving like kingfishers from century-old plane trees, and now and then a burst of pure, quavering Persian song, even more poignant in a Turcoman throat.

In Hamadan, while on the way to an already visited monument (he likes its dead end mountainside isolation), as we round a bend you hear a drum, and then over the drum a loud dissonant pipe. It is a Kurdish encampment, you are sure you can see women in tribal dresses dancing in a circle before the white tents. You ask him to stop. When he utters back only a nasal, "Why?" and lets the car roll on, you say, brutally, "What else am I here for!" and leap out.

When some hours later you return, sated by the bangled, eyes-closed women's dancing, the series of impromptu stick dances that had old women and even a policeman intervening, there is your friend maniacally polishing his hubcaps. He has wanted to spare you the jolting ride back by three-wheeler taxi. However, it is clear that your outburst has put you in the ranks of the clowns. For this he won't ever forgive you.

Isfahan-Kerman

There are certain days when the turquoise air of a Persian city becomes still and white. These days the airplane does not fly. If one asks when it may one gets only a smile, that phrase of the conversation manuals, "Come back tomorrow and we'll see." For the traveler who has run out of hotels willing to put up with him and his intestines for another night, this obviously won't do. So when his fellow ticket-holders—a plump personable doctor from Shiraz on his way to Kerman "to make his fortune", his mother, and his wife of three weeks (perhaps even more beautiful than the Taylor he insists on comparing her to)—propose that they hire a car, he blithely assents, glad of this opportunity to see something of the 500 miles of essential Persia that lie between Isfahan and Rugland's capital, Kerman.

Well, he is mistaken. There is nothing; maybe an occasional white-robed dervish standing silently by a cross-road imploring alms; or a series of pigeon towers; every thirty miles or so, a chimerical village announces itself through a screen of fruit trees, their pinks, whites, lime-whites peeping out like some astonishing sherbet. At irregular intervals the irrigation system's air-holes appear, bunches of hat-shaped mounds making a giant's drunken stagger across a plain the color of eggplant.

Five miles out of Isfahan the tar ends. From now on there will only be a gravel track, or hard-packed sand with perhaps a previous tire-tread that one follows like a piece of sky-writing. Here and there a great lunar stone juts and the road takes a serpentine swerve. The rim of eroded mountains stretching on up the valley gives a curiously sea-bottom feeling. Everything around you is silent. Then you notice that, though the speedometer registers 60 m.p.h., and the road is climbing, the ignition isn't on and hasn't been for the past half-hour. Obviously there must be quite a wind using your bags on the rack as its sail.

In Nain, at a roadside teahouse, lunch is served. Thick greasy soup into which bread flaps are sunk; new curds; whole chickens no bigger than the hand; tough, but tasty. We eat jackal-style, squatting in two facing rows on carpets from which the last sleepers have been evicted. Everyone stuffs as if it were his last meal. Back in the car and headed south now, we understand. We are in a duststorm. To our right we can see the mounds gathering into a corkscrew until, a sufficient height reached, they let themselves swirl off in acre-size bounds across an all but invisible landscape. We might be on the edge of a crater.

From time to time forms emerge; a man leading a string of moth-eaten camels, or a group of villagers in white facemasks plodding off in some unknown direction. Before long it becomes apparent that the car has a leaky radiator. Every time water is sighted the driver hops out with his pail while dust swirls and he wipes his hair and curses. At gas-stops the villagers collect: wild-eyed little children; apathetic dogs with chewed ears; one man with an advanced case of Parkinson's disease stands in one spot and shakes for us. While the radiator gurgles softly we reach into our pockets and take up a collection. As we near Yezd the villages begin to change. Wind towers with long tufted shafts appear and the villagers now sport turbans instead of caps.

With night the wind dies. Blue ripples lie across the road, which every now and then takes an unexplained swerve like some yawn one barely catches. The chauffeur drives like a banshee; on the left where there is less chance of catching a wheel, his tall figure outlined against the evening by the blue of his denims. To keep him awake, we supply him with matches. As the hours go by he works his way through box after box, lighting them and then throwing them away.

Towards midnight we pull up at a Rafsenjan roadhouse, the Hotel Asia. With Kerman still several hours south it seems wise to try to eat something. Moreover, the wind is blowing again.

While the doctor and his wife argue about whether to go on—I have a vision of her coming back, the grin of a first victory on her face—the driver takes his food out to the car. When we emerge an hour later he is asleep across the front seat. That settles it. It is arranged the men will sleep in one room, the women in the other. The doctor worries over his sheet. After much discussion he succeeds in exchanging it for one of fewer holes. The room itself is an inch deep in dust. When everyone is supposedly asleep, the doctor's mother gets up, proceeds to one of the corners and urinates; then, stepping gingerly, like a Persian Lady Macbeth, goes back to bed.

Next morning in a continuing duststorm we arrive in Kerman to be lodged at the inevitable Hotel Sahara. Completed six months earlier, it is showing signs of disrepair. Half the plaster has vanished and the floor is awash in dust. Spanning the room is a thin metal rod of the kind associated with neckties. It is, one understands, what keeps the domed ceiling from collapsing. To the Persians investing, what counted, obviously, was the garden with its nasturtium-ornamented pool, one side of which consists of a bare stone terrace flanked by colonnades of alternating pine and cypress, their long broom tips whistling as the soft wind bends them back and forth. The rest is a mishmash of fruit trees, threaded here and there with white-trunked pistachios (Kerman's other export).

Apparently no one before us has ever come to Kerman for his pleasure. We keep being asked if we are going on. To our looks of bewilderment come back names like Bam, Zahedan, Karachi, of the fortnightly bus and thousand mile gobs of glistening sand. Perhaps this is what has attracted me, a city at the end of everything that makes carpets: ugly ones, all pile, intended for America; and for Teheran, ones in which the design consists of a fanatically repeated single teardrop.

More to my taste are the merchants' own factory palaces with their jonquils and irises set in swelling carpet-medallion patterns; tall-columned porches whose arched doorways rise in an intricately receding series of white-on-white. Interiors are relatively simple: a few win-

27

dows of colored glass in peacock design; gracefully moulded stalactite ceiling corners (the one element of design mud domes permit); and everywhere vases of perfectly enormous blue irises. The final note comes from the red-embroidered shawls that one finds draped on chair-backs or made into room-dividers. They had been Kerman's main export until supplanted by the carpet industry in the 1930's.

Apparently none of the houses goes back much beyond 1900. In fact, very little managed to survive the two Afghan wars (almost apocryphal is the Agha Mohammad—the founder of the Qajar dynasty and an eunuch—with his tax of 10,000 eyes; he is said to have had them laid out in piles, then counted them himself). The oldest palace houses the ex-Point 4 mission. To its Americans it's obvious why we have come—to spy on them (but for which agency?). They think of Kerman as like their native Indiana. But they won't say which they prefer.

More amenable is the Assistant Governor-General, a man with nose so misshapenly huge as to seem the essence of his tribe. On our first day he has us summoned into his suite for tea and cakes. While we sip and scatter crumbs he fiddles with the blurts and squeaks of his short-wave radio. He is obviously lonely (four brothers and a sister live abroad, there is only his mother left in Teheran). He has spent the last two years in Bushire, on the Persian Gulf. There at least he could watch television. Here there is only the odd letter, like the postcard he hauls out of a friend with a big smile on his face surrounded by cabaret dancers. The picture, he keeps trying to explain, is a put-on. But what if it were real, if he could believe in a luck capable of conjuring them for all of a smiling second onto a roll of film—long enough to accept the momentariness of his fate.

That there are towns out beyond Kerman, we realize next morning when, after breakfast, the bell-hop mut-
ters something about Mahan, that magical name. Be-
witched, we follow him into the room of an enormous
German-speaking lawyer from Teheran, Aladdin S. On
the spot he offers to drive us there to see the shrine of
Sheikh Namatullah, Sufi mystic and poet. Nattily arrayed
in golf cap and loose flowing shirt, he seems with his fair
skin and his camera and transistor radio more German
than Persian.

We pile into a small taxi along with three other
Kermanis. Asked what they do, they say they are Jungle
Bunnies, meaning they work for the Jangalbani, or forestry service. Accompanying them is the office chauffeur,
thin as a monolith, and sad because there isn't room for
his aunt! The Persians seem completely unaware of any
element of discomfort. Energetically talking, laughing, in-
dulging one another in puns, they sit in each other's laps
and tickle each other's ears.

Through Aladdin we converse with our compan-
ions in the back seat. They include Mr. Nadji, a tall man
with wide-set eyes and a jackal's long thin face peering
from above a sunflower-red tie. Somewhere between his
legs sits he of the yellow tie, Mr. Vali, actor, poet (compared by Nadji to Mr. Sa'adi and Mr. Hafez), and now
forestry official.

In Mahan we find ourselves led through a series of
modest interconnecting gardens. In one, a trio of garden-
ers squats on hands and knees weeding the foot space
above which rises the branches of a little apricot tree. Already assembled are the Vali and Nadji wives, along with
Mr. Vali's two small sons and married daughter, a pretty
creature in black-and-white beach pants and yellow
blouse, with blacked-out eyes and a pile of henna-red
hair.

It is agreed that the apricot tree will provide the needed shade. With its green fruit as counters, a game of bingo begins. Carpets are spread out and chairs are brought for us men, leaving the women huddled in a volley of reds at the carpet's edge. As we play, a sense of strain makes itself felt, and a murmur goes up from the carpet-huddlers to the effect that sitting on chairs isn't very Persian.

After some minutes of this the men decide that a brisk tour of the shrine might be in order. With its simple white-washed interior and series of cypress-dotted courtyards opening one into the next (each with an octagonal pool and border of similarly octagonal pavestones), it for once manages to fulfill Granada's promise. After admiring the spreading petal design of the ivory-carved doors (brought across from India in the 16th century), we let our socks taste the thick oranges, blacks, indigos of an Afshari carpet. Following this we climb a swaying blue-tiled minaret from which Aladdin takes pictures, hundreds, half of them with us lending ourselves to the perspective out over the sloping oasis. We conclude that, since picture-taking is for Moslems a sin, it becomes a form of pleasure in whose name the Persian will go to any length, even that of escorting two perfect strangers across several hundred miles of desert.

When we return from the shrine, dinner is ready. Everyone takes off his shoes and squats on the carpets. There are platters of rice served in great conical mounds, *sabsi pelao* (dried fish and rice with spinach added), curds, two sorts of chicken, eggplant. As more dishes and bowls keep arriving, the diners sally daintily across the carpets to pour themselves glasses of red-tinted "whiskey" and scoop rice into their soup bowls.

After dinner, bingo begins, Mr. Vali's family winning one round after another. To celebrate, Mr. Vali gets up in his yellow undershirt edged in blue (the outer garment has been spilled upon and is on a line recovering), and, standing behind the apricot tree, plays old melodies on his shepherd's flute, his top knot of dark hair flopping gracefully as he tootles away and later recites his poetry. These are comic pieces, one to his invisible wife (with the refrain, "If you're going to go, go!"); another, a long ode to the no less invisible *jangal* which results in much laughter and slapping and glasses of whiskey.

At this point the Persians decide that our excursion would not be complete without a side-trip to Bam, a date oasis lying 150 miles to the south. We climb steadily through a wan, yellowish-green until we are met near a pass by a storm of locusts: the size of hummingbirds, but with doubled wings that make them look like tiny biplanes as they crash in smears of yellow over the windshield.

Bam itself makes an outlandish impression, with its rows of date palms, its narrow looping streets flanked by tall (20-24 feet) rounded cinnamon-red walls through which we drive looking for the house of the Provincial Agricultural Minister. He himself is at the *hammam*, but a squint-eyed serving woman with white tribal veil over her head appears bearing a jug of water. Through the door behind her we can see the moulded plasterwork of the interior with its stalactite-decorated dome. Her broad smile and manner make us want to snap her pouring water across her knee. Despite the absurdity, she poses, exploding with laughter when Mr. Vali aims at her his small transistor radio. Then with Aladdin in tow we set out to explore the gutted castle on the heights. In the setting sun, it seems less a mud-hued Carcassonne than the original for a Douglas Fairbanks Jr. film. Even more exotic are the date palms, their exploding greens relieving the squat rectangularity of the mud-baked dwellings.

Afterwards we repair to the house of another forestry official; to be regaled with quantities of tender gauze-skinned oranges, pistachios, loukoum candy, and of course the famous alcoholic black dates. We assemble in a long white room where we sit on little gilt-edged chairs furnished with cushions of red plush. Midway through the repast our host presents us with a great box of dates. Whereupon to everyone's delight Betty announces that it is her birthday. Endless glasses of tea are refilled and we stay on, greedily plopping dates into our mouths.

The way back is a horror, not only because it is night and night is evil, but because of the dates which have begun to resolve themselves into a desperation that each mile, each wayside stop, only increases. Let the Persians play their alphabetical poetry-quoting games (the way we as children on long car trip would play geography); let Mr. Vali lower his head and intone some of the great Sa'adi lyrics with their intense, bone-rattling stops, their lilypad explosions of vowels and dark crow-quavering spaces. It doesn't any longer matter. You know that something in you will collapse and it won't be a tire, but your intestine. The immediate occasion may be the only truly fine meal we will have had—in Aladdin's palace back at the end of many more miles and days in Teheran—chickens boiled and baked, bourbon, unctuous rice, nuts, watermelon, honey, cakes and a thick soup that spells water, gravy, hands; those of these two wonderfully fat (svelte pre-marriage pictures of a year ago are displayed) self-centered people now serving you.

Back in your hotel, listening to the thud of cars, of servants in the early morning beating rugs, you know, yes, you know that you will never see Meshed with its terrifying pilgrims, or Herat only 150 miles and three plane changes away. A doctor, old and French-speaking, is summoned. To his tune and savage, shattering pills there come servants from the house of your one friend, bearing armloads of yellow-colored broth. Somehow they all succeed. Your private piping no longer audibly rattles. You and your bags are hoisted into a taxi and swept out to the airport, past the remembered pestilence of porters and attendants with their grinning (how disinfected?) vaccination needles; past and into a space where little squat towns spread like jig-saw puzzles against patches of green and unfarmed desert—and, in the east, white amphitheatrical mountains. When some hours later you land, it is to be struck by the paradisiacal luxury of this European city, Istanbul, with its green rolling hills, its estuaries and dark heavy trees: all like an unnecessary incense, like something wrapped in a veil and given the name of woman, but which isn't that, is simply a mirage—a music—with drums and under the wrists white tiny bells, the one music you absolutely must have.

PANEGYRI: LESBOS

MORNING SHOULD FIND US SOME-
where by a Greek port, a pair of sailors in their
summer creams signifying the dream that it is;
or the red lobster of a cafe sign pointing towards the heat
of a few hours hence. As we round its rim, the port spills
forward in sea inks, in house tones aswim in the quick,
bougainvillea-alive shadows; patched yellow or pure white
testifying to the then or now of Piraeus or island. Island,
we decide, so much calmer, more eternal, and the camera
flickers over to that shade of the dial, easily as a washing
machine turning a degree on a program knob.

Here ropes are more in demand, an oily sun
strikes cardinals of flame from mast and water. All seems
ready to levitate, white of a pigeon gracefully flying over a
field. So, from that followed hovering, should we take in
the shadowed house cubes before dropping on a clean,
color-lit beach: perfect water; perfect face of a man sub-
merging that stooped part of himself, the laving stuff
coming up to his wine-purple knees. We hear the colors
of the waters. We hear the flying of a great piece of
toast—a boat in air! Little houses loom, we see them in
the undersplash from right below the boat's bottom,
swimmer's perspective. Then all is lost in the yellow of a
wine glass, a table napkin's white, a cafe perched so high
that the island thimbles seem lost in pale, silvery-blue
mist. In the quiet, in the sunshine, a music strikes up,
santour-thin entrance into the dance of the days.

Perhaps we can see these days as they stretch
forth in walks, in the soft blues of the hen-scurrying,
pomegranate blossoming courtyards: blocks, holes, sudden streets where time stays white like a burst of shadow.
But these, for all their beauty, should be seen as a series
of rapid, rapid cuts against which the music taps, louder
and louder, its urgency.

When we can stand it no longer here is a panegyri. We know it by a bigger crowd than we have ever seen before: mules and donkeys strapped to pines and doorways, a gigantic procession wending somewhere—to a hilltop church, a sky. Up over the gravestones, up above the sea, in the close-packed pink or blue house-echoing lanes we follow them, Eisenstein's faithful; then through the candle-lit sanctuary, each man, woman, holding one against his moustached, serious face. Vendetta colors. Old knickered men in their various mufti, turbaned and waterpipe smoking; others in snowplow moustache on a horse, their revolutionary violence figured in the tsamiko and klephtics of the background music, in the flashing, flashing white shirts and fierce, fierce faces.

Events are exploding like sundust, pink and lilac share the air, violet is all about under the awakening trees, we are elsewhere island-wise, but it is the same linked dancing, four brothers, two sailors, only the chapel background is black-and-white gaslamp chiaroscuro and we are more aware of still-life contents: soup, cheese, rush flasks; a music as liquid, dodecannese soft, as in the first stringed sequences. We are back where we began, even if it is no longer night but rose morning, returning handwalkers' song echoing up through the trees to where, perhaps, even ourselves may be found, stripped of trousers, still shirted, heads in each other's necks in what must seem the longest of mornings held, silvery sun-soft rising. Smiles become memories, memories shadows. Cliff I lie with, pencil myself deeper, whiter, into.

□

A fishing village set near the mouth of the highly saline Dardanelles could not help but prosper. Since the Romans of Longus's time various conquerors had come, Franks, Venetians, Turks, but the good life afforded by the abundant olive groves and fertile pastures had remained marred only by increasing dryness.

Then had come the 1923 catastrophe with its wholesale uprooting of what had been until then an inseparable culture. You put down a line, one with anywhere between three and twelve miles of strait in it. You called one side Turkey and the other Greece. Then you forbade all but the foolhardiest fisherman (with sheep to steal in the eyes and a horde of screaming children at home) to make a crossing that for three thousand years was any Greek's to make.

So, a lively trading center had become this faded, edge of Asia art colony village. It hugged to its chest the brittle pastel of its past and there it sat like an old, many-petalled rose. It supported but some fifteen hundred souls. It couldn't seem to find its knees. When with the help of basket and cane it did get down to market, there was always the problem of tottering its way back up the steep needle-comb streets. Whoever possibly could, left—for Germany, America, and Australia. Whence the money orders returned, leaving a society of pensioners to play a checker game with the rooms and screened-off corners of an intended's home.

On Kaldis's recommendation we had taken rooms at a new government-run hotel a mile or so outside of Mythymna. As the weeks went by there I came to feel as if I were choking. I kept asking if the bikinis and resort mentality were ever penetrated by *rebetika*—two men, heads bent, cigarette in mouth, at opposite ends of a huge wooden circle weaving to a bouzouki—but the foreign-speaking people I asked, the mailman, the mayor, of course responded that there was no such thing.

I had been there a fortnight when the mayor organized a folk dance demonstration in honor of a visiting American destroyer (sufficiently armed to blow up the whole Eastern Mediterranean, the captain proudly told me). For it, musicians and dancers were imported from the mountain village of Aghiassos, a half-island away; indication, it would seem, that no one in Mythymna cared; a view somewhat belied by those locals seen afterwards dancing among the pulled-down bleachers. For them the show was more than a publicity stunt. The music, the smells of grilling souvlakia, conferred festivity; enough to make them want to dance to their own hand-clapped rhythms. Still, I would no more have believed in it as an omen than I would have believed in some contemporary Russian peasant revolt. Of the island villages Mythymna was practically alone in not having a panegyri or saint's day festival. And the one panegyri I had seen so far, at Kalloni on Saint John's Day, seemed more like an American church fair with horse races, expensive beer, tangos, and boring circle dances. The Anatolian amane or passion wasn't evident.

For those first weeks I was in no position to worry about amane. I could barely walk. The heat and the blinding reflections prevented most goings and comings; all but the trips down to the beach to stare sullenly out at the scummy gray-green water, while acquiring a tan that might allow me to walk.

Gradually I learned to relax; or, since Greeks are among the world's more nervous people, to give the appearance. Now and then I'd catch a bus into the island capital, four hours of jolts and passengers vomiting and bays so agonizingly blue that my eyes smarted as they would from smoke. The noon sun was frighteningly real.

For five hours everything came to a halt. Not a phone rang. Only a dazed rooster somewhere tottered. Everything was pale yellow stubble; not the electric clarity of Attica, but an opaque Asian torpor of alkaline wastes here and there set off by an olive grove or stand of pines. Even the blue of the sky didn't give relief. Unlike the Cyclades, there were always clouds about, hemming in with their opaque, Asiatic mystery.

I had been there almost a month seeing Kaldises wherever I went when one evening the master himself, shaggy shepherd sweater, twelve-foot-long crimson scarf "knit by the thousand virgins," turned up at our hotel. Took one long look at the surroundings over dinner before querying in his gruff fashion, "How can you, a poet, be living a mile out of town in this pseudo hotel? You'll never get to see the real Lesbos here. You should stay in town."

For a moment I was speechless. Wasn't it he who had directed us here? But what he was saying so corresponded to my own feelings that I decided not to risk getting him off on a tangent. Instead I asked, "How can we stay in town? There are no hotels."

"Why stay in a hotel? All you need is to rent a couple of rooms in someone's house." And he proceeded to tell us about this pasha's palace where he and his sloe-eyed Nota were staying: deliciously cool two-story-high rooms with painted ceilings and shuttered views looking out towards Turkish Troy; the prettiest garden in town with almond trees and serpent mosaic floor; not to mention an orchard with a flock of sheep and goats. "The miscreant who owns it," he went on, "is a retired police force colonel. He is said to have collaborated with the Germans. He and his wife, the ex-pasha's daughter, help support themselves by renting out rooms."

"Are there any available?" I asked.

"There's a pair that would suit you and your family across the hall from us. Why don't you come over tomorrow afternoon around five and see. I'll give Betty a painting lesson and you can write a famous poem about it."

Next afternoon on the balcony overlooking the Colonel's garden I found Kaldis huffing about in his bathing trunks: a great pot-bellied bear of a man, with deep juniper-craggy eyebrows and a large scalpel-like nose on which a wart's fig-tree of hairs figured prominently. "Where have you been all this while? Making love?" The sally delivered, he turned, slapping his belly for emphasis. "Look at this splendid physique of mine. No one would say I was sixty-three." In actuality all this banter was a smokescreen to disguise his own unpreparedness, his lack of even a brush. But then he wasn't here this summer to paint, but to write his memoirs.

Our watching Kaldis as he painted, a canvas tacked to a cardboard box in place of an easel, reminded him of watching Matisse in his Nice studio, the color values changing with each stroke like a game of soccer. Only for Kaldis, a Greek, a painting was a spool to be unravelled, gingerly, strand by colored strand, out of the Platonic sky of his conception.

Taking a dab of red on his thumb he implanted the kiss of a poppy field next to some martial olive. A few more strokes, a pair of knee-like rocks, and, at the bottom, a bay's oversized starfish.

There remained only to look at it upside-down and on its side as he placed it in the balcony's half shadow, then against the full cream of his bedroom wall, seeking which of his three possible categories it would fall into, "work of art," "masterpiece," "miracle." Followed, calmly, by "Five hundred dollars" and a title that would grow ever more mysterious, "Sappho's Dream," "Polychromatic Wood."

Next day we moved into the Colonel's. The palace had its drawbacks, not the least being its owner, pink-faced portraits of whom, in sword and full-length military regalia, hung all over our second floor hall. Retirement hung heavy on him.

When he wasn't sitting on the porch in his baby-blue pyjamas, he was likely to be turning off our taps, or provoking curdling screams from the twelve year old servant girl, his shepherd's daughter. As a result of domestic economy (conserving bread by turning it into delicious pastry), his wife had grown rather massive and, as he said plaintively in his high-pitched French, "Who can make love to a bulldozer?"

□

As I accompanied Kaldis about, up one or another street picked more for its chance of shadow than any directness, I learned his story. Born in Turkish Dikeli, he had moved to Lesbos at the age of nine, remaining until sixteen when he ran away to join an uncle in Alexandria who was in the cotton shipping business. After three years spent mostly at sea, he had come to New York, settling in Hell's Kitchen on the lower East Side. It was a difficult area to prosper in, sleeping in shifts in a flophouse, while educating himself in the public libraries. How he got into union work I don't know, but during the depression he helped Diego Rivera organize the hotel workers. Rivera, in turn, encouraged him to paint—small canvases the size of a forearm. That left the rest of his considerable person free to concentrate on his self-publicity, that bohemian figure to be encountered any evening at the Cedar Bar or by the door among the coats and red-and-winter purpled faces of a gallery opening.

On the lecture circuit Kaldis was wont to talk about the "Restless serenity of the artist in his studio." In his own person "serene restlessness" might have been more apt; unable to sit in a cafe without bellowing at some passing nymph, "Beauty, come sit down!" When Beauty, to her own surprise, found herself drawing up a seat—age, after all, has its privileges—he might add in his best artist's manner, "You have lovely eyes and thighs," with outstretched paw rubbing the latter as if they just might be blue or green. Followed by a further flash of paw, "Those panties, how much you pay for them?"

The beauty isn't a New Yorker, she won't say. Undeterred Kaldis feels them. "Not silk are they? Why not? Silk too expensive for you?"

"Yes, I work for a living."

Fatal mistake with Kaldis to reveal the vocal chords. In a jiffy he pounces, "Oh, so you're not an artist, are you? You've got no man to support you. Your Daddy's not rich?"

"Oh, yes, he's rich. But he doesn't want to support me."

"So, you're an heiress," Kaldis rejoins, hands punning insolently among the long tresses. "What does your Daddy do, own supermarkets?"

Bit by bit he would drag out the whole spoiled, sheltered story, seeing whether he could enroll her in that exclusive sorority, the Daughters of Kaldis. To him a woman was a castle, waiting to be assaulted. And it was only the prospect of that assault that got the blood once more coursing through his piratical organ.

With Kaldis about to explain history, or how a poplar grew—by jetting a bubble into the sun and leaning on it— a certain contentment stole over me. I even forgot the rebetika for which I had come. What concerned me was the round of a day, how the landscape got up, dressed itself, and was. And mercies spread, gold soft mountain ring I held.

□

Awakening.

Time, new here, waits. Child-yellow field cuffs glow.

The first rose, I feel, is about to be born.

Then silence. Then what, a green hen?

Walking down, I watch the fishing boats dance into stone pockets of shore. In the soft light a villa's white-tubed, pink-roofed outline swims drunkenly, all by itself.

Axe-shaped hills rise and, stuttering, a line of pauses leaps towards a blue repose of yet vague houses and, below, a silk-clean sea.

There, at the edge of vision, three headlands float, each of their shadow naps a giant leaf which, as it strikes, makes a gong.

□

Shoelaces appear—and go away again. Beaded curtains out of which the men advance, plastic beads tucked in slim, behind-the-back-held fingers.

They hold their lies stretched in each other's pockets. They make roosters vanish with their calls.

Sunfry shirts. Orange suspenders. A donkey draws up and on he jumps to ride down a dung-yellow street and out where no breakers tumble. Just stubble, a peasant landscape's small butterblue houses, waiting. For this flask of a shirt to come and tie his goat to a pail, his house to the lid of the morning, where it coughs once, drunkenly.

□

In the town shop gratings are clanking open. The grocer is green-aproned. With his voice he holds out all he contains and tosses it. Up and down.

Up where brooms splash in the new silver of a courtyard.

Soft water down. Tree and ladder down. To earth. To me, colored by an hour that wears a green apron. Lifting its kerchief I watch it sing, softly—for the wind in its almond branches. Like hay and I, high, on it over a stubble white as the peasant threshing below with his one or four round-circle horses. I watch. My hands have become a butter, that golden! And the earth over which they turn is an earth where each thing stands in its tall cone, wears its smile like the purest of sun-hawk glasses. I swim. You, Betty, draw up your knees and wave.

□

The old man has his baggy knickers on, his whiskers curled. Around his middle is a yellow sunsplash of a cummerbund. Later it will turban his head as somewhere far below he turns in the slow yoke of the threshing.

I see him as the essence of roundness. Not earth so much as that well by which he sits in his round keg-like boots while, gloppity-glop towards him, comes the true master of things here, donkey. His sovereign stands there

now, dominant, rush hampers gleaming like a large
moustache.

□

The late morning strikes and rolls towards me a
white. Bell. On its bubble of sound I walk through the
town gate and out where noon rages like a turkey in the
long wicker grass. Here, if darkness lives, it is as spade,
as sparrow. As the black basket shapes of these field
women. Stooped. Cutting from under the edge of their
sorrow whatever is—stalk, voice, star—and sewing it in.
Like bread itself. Or flowers, a huge, lapbright bunch.
Sign how a traveller could have felt welcomed: *you have
come into our land, may it bring you joy.*

With my tribute I set off down a black, bending,
bicycle and tree-lined road. Color calms me: the donkey
carts with the lacquered blue dolphins; these bits of pink
villas, faded, like cake-icing. The port, its houses strung
above a pocketwatch confusion of masts and bobbing
caiques. Narrow streets mount like vines.

Hands in the sun, fishermen squat, repairing folds
of yellow netting. Everything else has a look of suddenly
bleached towels in whose heat only the bewhiskered push
their carts.

Secrecies of air: wine and flies.

In the shadowed courtyards silence flicks its
broom, backwards, forwards. Blinks. Raises its head, its
donkey eye. Passes the last bright grape through its
mouth and lies there, chest calm, feet color of smoke, and
hair, the very happy hair, still.

□

When days are too long you have to go somewhere with them. One charm of a Byzantine culture is
that wherever you go it will be somewhere your size.
Shape of a hat, body of a pencil pulling up before these
cafe awnings with their jacketed, crab-scurrying waiters.
Or inside where the ceiling comes in peaked wooden
beams and everything is pale blue and photograph-
festooned: royalty; heroic whiskers; on the marble tops,
water. Water and card slap. Further away reflections,
shirts, wool suits, elaborate whiskers, astrakhan hats.
Waiting in their frayed clothes for something. The next
earthquake.

"I like you, come sit with me."

Like the idiot, the stranger you are, you accept.
He is the pilot, you the shoal. No, he is a jewel case you
hold. His name is George, fifty-sheep-he-owns-them-
George. He is nuts about rebetika and dances hypnotical-
ly as you know, having one evening surprised him and his
cousin, Strato, in the fishermen's cafe, cigarettes in hand,
circling to a zembeikiko. One of these days, he says, he
will rent you his mare and you will go off together to
some panegyri, some spot of music in the island
somnolence.

Off he goes to his six-kilometer-distant corral and
the afternoon turns on its slow, sun-split hands.

□

When later I wake there is still sun, flowering here
in a house's morning-gloried peace, there an air of too

many chickens, and on the stoop beside them these two beautifully old and walnut-bright faces.

And the afternoon liquidity rides. Soft blue against the letters of the trees. White and gold where my invited, jam and fork eating self sits, trying to imagine what it must feel like to be so many feet from a dowry's end: that red and budlike nail in the hourglass dusk quivering.

Start. And stop. And let the needle in. And count. And make something small and bent and like a tree with goatpaws in it like laughter tipped. Then in the quick day-end walk, thinking of those who have already emigrated where a girl does not have to wait for spring and a veil of white blossoms to offer herself.

Turn, reassemble, and now with your friends, three abreast, parade among the churn of red, nickel-screaming bicycles. Or pause and talk to a kid whose legs bend from a wall. Count on the mouth of the wind horses—that mane and tail stretched, olive-shaking grove. Then let brightness shine, brightness that is more than their own blue, tossed, sea-cantering shapes; more even than bay with chaff like so much ikon gilt upon it; so bright that only in moonlight can it truly glimmer and become *tsiftetelli*—two sailors, arms twirling over the head, fast-legged, dancing it. Dreaming of whatever the dolphin in them dreams—a Mytilini tart with breasts that tinkle bells and a huge guitar of an ass.

□

When the day has finished screaming, when the last goat and fence has retired, time (old man who wears his white trousers low) comes, takes off his things of salt, and writes.

You are in your socks not far from him asleep.
The world and the beast in you have separated. Only sad-
ness is, like a calm, quiet pudding.
Put it in your hand now and go.

☐

By early August I had come upon a number of
shepherds who were, like George, zembeikiko fanatics,
willing to talk about it and, when the spirit moved them,
to dance. They weren't able to teach me because that
dreamlike zig-zag striking requires *kefi,* something that
must well from within. (This is why few Athenians know
how to dance it.) But now and then in their company I
would totter forth from a table, improvising out of what I
had observed. The strongly-accented rhythms did the
rest, providing a containing circle within which I could
look over my shoulder and copy, or answer back. But I
had no way of dancing for myself, nor any desire to.

☐

Mid-August, time when panegyris are bursting
forth almost daily from the pent woodwork of a summer.
For the Feast of the Virgin, George and I have resolved
to go to Aghiassos, as its folk troupe would indicate that
there at least people dance. Unfortunately, the night
before, Betty decides we should give our own end of summer party: with violin and accordion (the village barber
and his brother), Beatles records, natives, foreign beards.
It seems at all times on the verge of a brawl. I don't get

home until 4 a.m. When I wake, four hours later, the one bus of the day has gone.

Undeterred, I tell Betty I'm going anyway. On my blue cork-soled beach shoes. And I point a hand in the direction of that two mountain-range away town.

"You're drunk. Why don't you stay here and go with us tomorrow to the panegyri at Petra."

I answer that Aghiassos is the island's prettiest village and that should make for a panegyri worth attending.

"How long will you be away?"

"Maybe two days—if the first is good."

"All I can say is that you'd better be at Petra, or I won't answer for the consequences."

With throbbing head and nothing but some reading matter and a bathing suit in a satchel I head down into the little dell where last night's expensive cafe looms. Over a needed coffee I ask about my cashmere sweater, flung aside in the midst of a dance. Not there, but the girl obligingly points to another, same general green, new on a hook. Proudly, forgetting the mountainside where I am headed, I turn it down and stamp off down the sweltering road towards Petra.

With each mile I grow more and more apprehensive: both of the sun and the increasing unlikelihood of coming upon a car or a motorcycle big enough to carry me over the switchbacks to Kalloni and the chance of a taxi. I am on the other side of Petra and starting to climb when I opt for a shortcut along a forest riverbed.

Immediately a whole new exhilaration fills me: of what it means to be moving, jumping, up through these mossy, handheld rocks, the path under me spinning gargoyles of pale, pointed color. Where the breath is the breath that licks to itself a stone: stone in which I, slow fish, swim.

When I emerge at last I see the road ahead mounting in a series of black, heat-reflecting coils.

Dreading it and the walk down on the other side in the treeless glare I decide on what I take to be another short-cut: along the hill crests to the mid-island market town of Aghiou Pareskevi, a town somewhat closer to Aghiassos, and one I have never been to.

What about losing my way? Well, as the crow elsewhere flies, so must here the donkey trot. When in doubt as to two paths I have only to take that where he lies thickest.

Before me nothing. Olives. Nothing. Olives. Occasionally cobbles. White and Roman-looking and going nowhere. Or a high, equally white, broken-neck bridge. But no houses—nothing that has a roof. And no people other than a surly peasant feeding a bag of small pears to his horse. And, hours later, the silver bell of a herdboy, asleep in his shirt under an olive.

Stones, hills, sunlight, olives. Strung like so many beads out over the blue. Throwing spoons of shadow into the air and catching them. Pretending it is all still here, First Time where I sit, the ring on the finger of the day, the smile in the ward, the white oven of its silence.

□

As I pick up my journey I am conscious once again of the sun settling over this one, hoof-white, donkey-dung stone gulley of a path. I feel the burning in my throat, calling me onto the fields that I have taken to for their softness; fences before each of which I must stop, lifting one leg, now the other, as one might a suit-case. I burn, I fidget with this bathing suit I've tied like a moth around my head, and on I come, the pathway below crookedly wavering like the whitest of sheep. That stupid, that much to be followed.

Finally in an hour that is just the dungshapes of horses asleep in a distance that glitters mice and hay-shaved stubble, I find it, that Quarter Mile Off The Road Farmhouse. Into its squatting, tobacco-separating family I burst, demanding in my best wolf tones, "Water." Which comes after a moment's hesitation—seven pure, silently-filled glasses. Then a melon, its white cap removed, and presented with a spoon. When I have gouged out the last green ounce, what can the family do but whisper something to the girl who has fetched me the glasses. Fearing it, the unrepayable generosity of the truly poor, I get up and, with a smile of thanks, trundle off in the pointed direction of Aghiou Pareskevi.

After an hour's walk along a white track that glitters like a lamppost I reach Aghiou Pareskevi. At this hour its blue-shuttered streets are empty save for two young men, arms around each other's shoulders, quietly, shyly bicycling. Further on, encountering a lady, I ask if she knows of a restaurant that might be open. Not only does she escort me all the way across town to the main square; but, to my astonishment, after pushing open the cafe's gates, goes behind the counter to dole me out a small icebox's supply of tomatoes and feta, and the water for which I must keep humbly asking.

A nap now? I am directed to an adjoining hotel. After being shown the five beds, I pick the one with the longest sheet: so soft, each time I adjust a cloud of dust puffs up, while a parade of flies struts in and out of my nostrils and along the pursed banks of my lips.

□

The country under me, half asleep, is that magical one that paintings inhabit. Where I am me, light. Light and roses, those about my horses' upturned trotting necks on the way to that great shrine, panegyri. Which beckons, open and bright. Open with peasants, with carts, with ikons and cakes and toys and shops. Bright with all the light that an orchestra, or three or five, can pour into it. I am Chicken Little and if the sky is falling, then call these fragments the pieces of my luck. Held outstretched before me like this glass and pitcher, this plate with its white cheese and black simple olives.

Should Time at that moment rise and hand me a wet clear spoon I would not look up. What is around me like clay, like olive trunk and shadow, is more than enough. So I watch and so the others, forms too of light, of new clothes and hair, stroll. Back and forth, talking to the quiet ditch, their neighbor's wife. Pressing hands in their wool trousers and standing there, just standing there, waiting for late afternoon when the music will begin.

As they circulate in that water-weave among stalls and trees that is any panegyri, any landscape gathered out of its work-day invisibility and pronounced human, I may begin to understand why I am holding this table. For what a panegyri gives in the course of a day's dancing may be nothing less than what Marx and Engels meant by the "withering away of the state." Only what in them is utopian jargon is this reality through which I have sunwalked and red-apple dreamed, and of which these celebrants are the human incarnation.

Not that this dissolution happens right off. The landscape, the ongoing four thousand year fact, must be first established. For this tradition decrees a horse race. Imagine a road dense with people, some even in the trees (by a field post, crouched on the flat of his hands, a photographer). Then in pairs, quick as a telegraph, flash percherons ridden bareback, Parthenon-frieze style.

With the first darkness comes more crowdedness, more tern-flash of waiters carrying round platters of shoeleather beef and expensive beer. And the orchestras begin, at first playing arranged medleys, then, with the coming of evening, dance tunes addressed to the individual paying dancers.

The floor now? Moonspit, white, strawless. Forms bow, spring, make their moonflicks and are gone, whence you can't say. In all of this there is intelligence: weaving movements; ironic matchflame fingers. Then, late, it may happen, that abolition of a landscape which is a peasant, alone on the great white of the floor, dancing his zembeikiko.

What will have impelled him onto the floor is hard to say. There will have been the long night, the music and its alcohol. Slowly in the course of it he will have felt something welling. With a half gallon of wine in his throat and feeling pressed, pressed with the kerosene of the orchestras and the whole worked strawchurning summer, he gets up, pockets his matches, and, with cigarette in mouth and his two women by him (the wife in a dumpy brown dress, the daughter in a sprightly red check), dances a folk dance. Ceremonially almost, for the benefit of the surrounding tables and every dead person within stamping range. When this bit of ritual is accomplished, he lowers his head and stands there, while all around the people, wife, daughter, friends few or none, fade away like dreams, like the parched rubble of stones, hens, and who knows what of his daily life.

He is there, standing. The music above him, a great black cross. As he starts to dance, he takes something up from his hand, looks at it, wipes it once across his trousers, looks at it again. Then with foot he says something that crashes on the floor like the word, "Spit." When the floor doesn't answer back, he takes his best palm and with it. HITS. Down across his life, across all that the books and others says he is: shoes, floor, black of nail, trousers. Hits, smashes. And the floor, like a wet green log, like all his face and trousers, flames. Flames and becomes the perfection of this ouzo glass that someone is now offering him. Together in the moonfloor silence he and the glass's one possible giver—his wife—drink. What he has been doing is plain. Setting fire to himself. And not only to himself, but to this landscape of which he is the shadow made flesh. Made hair and bones and forty-eight years of age and now, grasshopper style, dancing. Creating spoon, fork, apple with a red center. Creating with every gesture something new, not of this world, and now by him, for the eyes of all within drinking distance, spun, twisted, erected. I am me, he says. I burn the knife. I cry.

Three-quarters of an hour later here I am stumbling out past a grinning hotelkeeper. In the square I come upon some youths, hair properly combed and a sweater folded over the shoulders. On an August 14th that can only mean one thing. "Aghiassos," I ask, going up to them, "how are you getting there?"

Small cups of smile, then finally a broad grin as understanding hits. A maroon-colored bus lying under an acacia is pointed out. Am I to understand that it will take us there later in the afternoon?

At 4:30 p.m. magical letters, "Aghiassos," go up, and to a burst of songs from the boys in the rear the bus leaves. The road under the olives like a ladle turning, dipping. Past fat, smacking, zlack! cigar-dust Kalloni plain. Where the color darts, stops, as the embroidering needle spins, and over fields makes. Swallows. Makes this glistening tobacco and horse-dotted plain through which the road winds, up over dale and down past. Hoes. Peasants by them, peering from soft petal-brim hats at an afternoon just their brick-colored shirts, their threescore oranges. Pop them against your throat, feel them bursting.

And donkeys. Long ones with dark skinny tails and spots and where-to-pin-it signs. Who look up as if you were finally going to, before lapsing back into their essential shrubbery.

The road, a music now, bends, dips back on itself, turns. Transparency is in its gown of fat bell-thick olives. Blue shadow goats here. A stork, black on white apron-wing upfluttering there. Or a roadworker, a red flower in his teeth, hand on hip insolently standing.

At an old oak tree crammed full of canes, umbrellas, girdles and bras dear to St. Anthony, we turn up into the Olympus range towards Aghiassos. Almost immediately you feel a new, decidedly sylvan presence as the bus swings in and past camped picnickers and rose-festooned, uphill-trotting carts. Finally, at the foot of the town, in a great beech-shaded square jammed with pilgrim buses, we are let out to walk, taste the sweetness of the mountain air.

As I walk up the cobbled street, the going is steep enough for eyes to explore: the back and forth of the fruit stands with their green huge "American" apples in hanging nets; jugs for sale and being bought by tourist-happy villagers; candy stalks everywhere; a visual bobbing feast that, even so, doesn't quite prepare me for the jam-packed motley of the cathedral yard, almost terrifying in the mass of its elements. I expect to be searched at the walled doorway. Instead there are girls selling white crosses. Elbow to elbow, the whole length of the cathedral rim, huddled figures lie, determined to spend this one night sleeping in sanctity.

After standing suppressed in a pushing, slightly steamy line I am admitted to the great clanging cathedral. Whole families are squatting on the marble floor, picnicking on chickens and chewing watermelons. While all around them a wonderful mob circulates: vendors of holy items; children jingling bells; bearded, mitre-hatted priests in pink robes abstract as stars.

Seeing a candle-holding line part company for the chanting priests, I decide to join it. Finally here I am by the glass-encased Ikon of the Miraculous Virgin. I plant my candle, stoop and kiss the sacred glass; to be re-warded with a sprig of basil, while a second lady squirts my spot with disinfectant.

With the sprig tucked behind my ear I head out into the comparative quiet of the night-fallen streets. In a large mall near the bottom of the town three orchestras are operating over what is, in each case, no more than ten round feet of floor, where one virtuoso couple after an-other dances and across which a continual succession of waiters stirs.

To me the dancing seems contrived: white-shoed types up from Mytilini to do their one, well-rehearsed number; then, since floor space is at a premium, shift to the next cafe where the exact same succession of dips, turns, leaps will be enacted. Dancing more because their image demands it than because for months they have been thinking of little else and it's either dance now or wait for another year.

For me, meanwhile, there is the pleasure of circu-lating, sitting wherever I can find a chair and exchanging English conversation for homemade bread and stuffed eggplant.

At 3 a.m., as I'm on my shivering way to the cor-ner of piled rugs I've rented, I run into two guests from our party of the previous evening. Their enthusiasm re-launches me. First, uphill to see if something might be go-ing on at the hilltop cafe. Then back down to the mall. We arrive just in time to witness a real peasant syrtos. Two old knickered men are dancing, or rather jumping, in what looks like a shower of offered ouzo, while to one

side a young blade in city clothes stands clapping, flamen-
co style.

For twenty minutes, tirelessly, as if dunking for
apples, the two go on. When they are through a young
man with a bit of sailor in him, (among his table of blades
I have noticed his pawing feet), stands up and executes a
magical zembeikiko. He follows it up with a fast, finger-
snapping tsiftetelli belly dance that has the surrounding
twenty-five of us gasping, faces lit in shy ecstatic smiles.

In full daylight to a virtual stampede of splendid
single dancers the orchestra goes on playing. And it is not
until seven o'clock that they manage to control themselves enough to call it a night. Even then there are men
still needing to dance whom for another half-hour I
watch, turning en masse before a jukebox. At that hour,
as we all know, anything works.

□

Hard to leave Aghiassos. Especially when the late
morning reveals more isolated dancers turning outside a
shop, a cafe's slanted cobbles. If a few are like this now,
what will the whole town be like by evening? I feel torn,
wanting to see what a sustained festival will offer, whereas
at Petra there will be dancers I feel closer to, having
shared their landscape.

To ponder it I go order some cakes in a pastry
shop—battle the yellow-jacket. He wants to kill himself, I
want my breakfast, let's see who wins. Fifteen minutes later it's the yellow jacket and I am headed down the blue-
balconied streets to the bus depot.

How to tell which bus goes my way? Does it matter,
since they must all go down the mountain and once at the
oak tree I should be able to fend for myself. With a po-

liceman's help I find one willing to let me off there. Only the junction comes, goes, and we are several turns below before the driver realizes that this freak indignantly tapping at his window panes is me.

On my tattered soles the road is a heat-reflecting bowl here and there enlivened by some down-walking festively-dressed peasants, or a gypsy couple, the man leading a small larva-like child slumped over a horse. Finally I'm back where the bus should have left me. On the left and shaded side of the Petra road are two ancient seat-white stones. Perched on one is a tall, moustached man with a shoulder-folded coat to show that he, too, was at last night's panegyri. To try out my Greek, I ask how long he has been there. An hour, the man replies, irritably. Once about every ten minutes a possible lift in the form of a car pops into view, only to veer off for Aghiassos. But this doesn't bother me, I need the rest and enjoy sitting on my stone, wiggling my feet in the afternoon sunlight. Sooner or later, I know, a car will come and we'll be able to jump out and flag it down.

The chance to put this theory to the test comes sooner than I expect. From the direction of Mytilini a jeep appears, headed uphill. Will it, or won't it turn? While various me's take bets, I hunch forward, ready to spring into the road. But I haven't actually moved and, when the jeep turns up the mountain, my companion, who has stood up, lets out with a fearsome pavement-rending stamp. Then he walks over and says something like, "When a car comes, any car, you get your body out in front of it, understand!"

Do I? Less the actual words than what a stamp of that sort, abstracted from the dance floor, inevitably means. Up to that moment my life, like that of any serious traveller, had been directed towards a passive transparency. It's not me, but life out there that I wanted to see shine through. Suffice to say I had no idea as to what exactly a man is. His word? O.K., but I would not have been able to say what made that word come out, here green, there blue. Now finally I understood that what makes a man a man is his strength. We may not all have the same; but that does not mean that we should not use what we have to smash the nonexistent, *because-I-say-so* world into its whatever fragments. The gestures may be totally negative. But, rendered absolutely enough, they become what any taverna stamp, brush or sweep of hand, is—a door thrust open.

We are both on our feet when, down the road from Aghiassos, comes the very Aghiou Pareskevi bus of the previous day. Same grins and handshakes and weathered faces, deep in their accumulated treasures, their stiff sides and winey yawns. For an hour through the olive groves we ride. Five miles from Kalloni, at the foot of the climb to Aghiou Pareskevi, the bus lets us off.

In an almost lavender early evening we walk: hawk and it is singing, field and it is flying, away from here, back to there. The eye stops, sits, becomes a breath of the sky, those horses' high, steam-whiskered tails. It is in that sky that, silvered yourself, you walk among the far-off shimmering of the white, cube-like farms, your companion telling you that should you miss the special bus for the Petra panegyri, he will give you dinner, then whisk you over the mountain on his motorcycle.

As you walk the dream detaches itself from his mouth: cigarette of a smile, stopped for, lit. Then a question, "Do you like grapes, figs?"

Seeing no harm I reply, "Yes." Whereupon here he is plunging across the field. He has three red dripping bunches of grapes cut when, thinking to help, I proffer my satchel. He hesitates an instant, then with an air of finality drops them in. It is only later, seated miraculously on the bus and unable to give them back, that I realize how much of the man's property I have appropriated.

Next day, when I pull out my notebook, I find most of my summer's jottings washed away.

Petra is crowded. Unable to find even a box to sit on near the music cafes I join the *volta* circulating along the waterfront. Endless movie where the same marriage hopes, the same baby carriages, whirl again and again into view. It has a rhythm that at first eludes me, caught up as I have been in another sort of haste. Walking is walking, one would think. Well, here it isn't, just as a siesta isn't sleeping. The idea is to go slowly as if musing, now turning to talk to someone, now stopping by a well to take a puff, while all around the dreamlife stirs: round-faced girls with black-beaded eyes and costumes perhaps only possible as thought out in the secret fastness of a dresser mirror, who stand expressionlessly conversing. Groups of walkers turn, reassemble, and now, arms linked, walk, rearranging themselves into more and more solid collections of white shirts matched to black hair, trousers, shoes. Walk, meet people, smile, what those minutes on any sidewalk after a church service are, here made this seaside civility.

Still, a panegyri is more than its volta. As I stand noting the various possibilities, each orchestra with its own long movie theatre of packed tables, its distantly flashing dancers, I may wonder how I am ever going to get close enough to see anything. Then I spot tables migrating through the packed throngs, fire-fly style. Not long before my head, pleased, is bearing one, legs in the air. I plunk it down right under the lip of the stage, under the nose of the shrilling clarinet, there where the finger-blast whistles have most knifeflash somersault of shepherd trousers, shirts, empty beer bottles, wan giddy smiles.

The world starts making sense. Retsina is called for. Nervously it might appear from my perspective, surprisingly and wonderfully to the table of half-drunk shepherds beside me. In the next moment a watermelon appears on their table. Hardly cut, divvied up, and here is a photographer, here is everybody, me included, arranged in a great horseshoe of lifted, grinning glasses: the cigarette, pearl-like, in mouth and the head up as in solemn, nineteenth century *palikari* poses.

When the last bulb has exploded, let the drunkest of the lot, short, with hose-thin shoulders and perfect straight teeth, stand up and ask me to dance (he has run out of partners). I agree on condition that I be allowed to drink the three bottles I need. I am somewhere near the bottom of the second when my friend, who has a bus to catch, stands up. Our first dance is a languid, walk-behind-and-gawk *politiko syrtos*, a dance to get me used to the floor, that it is there, that I can be calm. In tribute, I suppose, to my foreignness I receive an exaggerated amount of ouzo, the dancing each time mercifully stopping as some shepherd stands up to proffer a glass. When it's over, my friend calls for his own wild, clarinet-filled tsamiko. It is the dance of his friendship, of all that he will do for you: pitch from your handkerchief: crawl between your knees, head tilted up star-wise and cigarette still squarely in mouth: followed, maybe, by a somersault from full standing position with only your kite-like handkerchief to hold him up. Not feeling up to such trust I ask one of his friends to replace me and sit down, knowing I must still make the long uphill-tottering walk home to Mythymna.

□

The summer is a great net I have pulled around me. In its last recesses I sit. With my reddened eyes I hold the sun. An orange goat ties me to his tree. When in ten days my flight leaves I should be ready.

But things don't work out quite like that. I may feel I need to be alone; in that way recover my sanity. But in Greece being mad is nothing, a whole segment of society is. This need only be declared for any number of volunteers to step forth, "Come, let me be your partner."

Three days after the Petra panegyri an Armenian husband and wife guitarist team arrived in Mythymna. They were hardly installed in the last of the rampart cafes when there was a *mikri* at the Colonel's door, "Music, George sent me."

With no choice, even though it is only four in the afternoon, I went, practically led by the hand to where, in the midst of a brick-skinned shepherd and fishermen lot, was the whole George family. With an empty seat as if specially saved and, not twenty feet away, the Armenian singing in one of those deep, old, belly-wobbling voices, its quarter-note *amanes* making that straw floor—part dream, part prayer—over which one or another dancer glides, bends, dips.

The Armenians remained anchored there for three blissful nights. When they left I felt I had experienced the Smyrna of Seferis.

A day later, as I dragged myself, soaked with sunlight and seawind, up the steps of the pension, I was met by a distraught George. It seemed that his striking eleven-year-old daughter, Eleni, whom we had engaged to babysit for our two-year-old son, had been sexually attacked by the Colonel. What the attack consisted of, an attempt to kiss her, a mild pawing, was unclear. But her convulsive sobbing had brought George, knife all but gleaming in its duty-bound scabbard up to our room. He regretted having let Eleni work for us. The Colonel was, after all, notorious. But he had thought that our presence as foreigners would protect her. "As it is, there is not much I can do. I'm a poor man." I was in no mood to lose our baby-sitter and I promised him I would do what I could.

The Colonel was nowhere in sight when I went out. But early next morning I found his baby-blue, pyjama-clad self pleasantly sitting in his garden chaise-longue.

"What do you mean," I said, speaking French, "by attacking that eleven-year-old girl?"

The Colonel laughed benignly. "It was nothing, nothing. Don't worry about it."

"Nothing?" I asked in the most mute of whispers. Then, after a moment's staring at the stone floor, I spat. Pointing to the chaise-longue to show that he was that spit, with a single stamp I ground my heel into it. As the Colonel recoiled, cringing, I added, "If you ever touch Eleni again, I'll not only denounce you as a war-time Fascist, but I'll come back and personally strangle you." With that I turned and walked back upstairs to my room.

That this bragadoccio succeeded had much to do with Kaldis. Was there ever a canvas to which a few flourishes couldn't be added? Miffed that he had not been on hand to take it in himself, he consoled himself by going down to tell the Colonel what an athlete he had sleeping under his roof. Whether this included a Golden Gloves pedigree I'm not sure, but it was enough to extract a payment to George for his wounded dignity, which allowed Eleni to return as my son's playmate.

A day later, by way of thanks, George asked if I would like to rent his pregnant mare and ride over to Magdalena for one last panegyri in honor of the saint who, year in, year out, for that one tall August 24th, shines. Saint Fun's day. Saint Drink 'Em Up's Day. Saint Black Vest and No Tie and the hair like George a whole Gray and Glistening Pomaded Olive Tree.

So take a piece of earth and beat sky, trees, wind into it. Beat a horse whose owner is this shepherd behind me in his jodhpurs and boots walking. Let our goal be those three headlands in the haze dimly, lionly, stretching. Mark on the longest of their forepaws a town. Call this the Nipples of the Magdalena and you will be as close to poetry as stone houses and pink-tiled roofs and lots of peasants sitting on their rush stools under grape leaves can get you. Not all that pretty, certainly, but then a town producing gangsters for Watertown, Mass. may be only bent on standing your hair on end; something I have experienced, having once previously passed on a horse through its rail-high, cafe-jingling sidewalks and trembled for my very stirrups.

It is mid-morning when we arrive. I have stopped to drink from the fountain by the town entrance when, from the cafe opposite, there comes some broken Australian, "What, my friend, are you doing here?"

I reply, "I'm here for the panegyri."

"You're out of luck. There ain't no panegyri today. Panegyri was last night. Many people, cars from as far away as Mytilini. But today there is nothing."

To let that sink in a bit further he invites us to sit down with him and sip some lemonade.

I accept only to find myself fending off the usual curiosity. How rich am I? How come I ride over here— not for the panegyri certainly! And he laughs his Australian laugh and talks about his hotel business back in Sydney, about everything but the panegyri which I see steadily disappearing, down the street, into the drugstore sun. Before it can get there, disappear utterly, I am on my feet, almost rudely parted.

Halfway into town the strap holding my saddle bag decides to give way. I have dismounted and am on my knees trying to gather up my effects when I suddenly become aware of this music, a music from back of the barn and the 3,000 B.C. sunrise, in dissonant brass exploding. Leaving everything to George (all day various of my odds and ends will be returned by anxious-eyed townsfolk) I head off towards what turns out to be a cafe's eight piece unelectrified orchestra: trombone, parade drum, accordion, bouzouki, guitar, violin, and over them, making the grape noise that hangs fat and purple on all the streets, clarinet. That long, that high up in the sky, pointed.

Inside with the band are some twenty middle-aged men in white shirts and vests and horse-heavy shoulders. The face bluish, upturned at the nose, and, if you want, Balkan-looking. With a mountain in it somewhere, that cliffside over which Magdalena and its whole intoxication of tiny shoebox cafes clings.

Into this, without a by-your-leave, I enter and in the obscurest corner root myself, saying, "Retsina, a half kilo, please, and some tomatoes." With the food come the attentions of a pair of urchins who don't know what to make of this man sitting all by himself at the blue window and poke straws in at him. But before all the evidence is in, the waiter has shooed them away. This leaves me in my corner, oblivious even of George (who will come in grousing, "How did you expect me to find you?" and, even more stupidly, "Why here?"), growing more and more my two hunched elbows, my refilled smile; wider as the dancing goes on, continuous poem and I'm writing it. On my shoes that want to, but don't know how.

It is late noon when the cafe, led by its owner, a great cloud of a man in white shirt and suspender-held gray flannel trousers, finds itself seized by the need for beauty; utter beauty, picture-album beauty, the whole party spilling out into the street in a handkerchief-linked file. Before a bemused assembly of canes and black-suited, whiskered, three-day-red faces they dance a *kalamatiano*. In the middle of the weaving rings the cafe waiter holds out a tray of tiny, opaque-white glasses. For the joy of the day they quaff. Then on in back and forth swaying circles they spin, leaving only the two of us and the band in the cafe.

Next cancel the town awnings with siesta: orchestra and dancers dissolved and the cobbles now just a lot of canerush stools filled with little men with black torn vests and shepherd crooks and plenty of sheep breath under their wool socks, plenty of red faces. Let George pick out as friend the reddest of the lot, who offers to find us kreas, "meat." When three butcher shops have somehow proved insufficient, he invites us to his own place in the bottom part of town.

Here in an unadorned cement yard, among circling flies, we sit, while the two women of the house remove our shoes and hand us, as gestures of welcome, sprigs of basil to be sniffed like a perfect martini. Soon even meat comes; for here, led in on a string, is a turkey. Nods of approval and some minutes later here again is the turkey, still on his two feet, but headless.

While the turkey is being dressed, the noon demands its own white sausages. Supply them and, while you're at it, lift up to the grape-trellised roof table, chairs, plates, and ouzo bottles. Have me in my clumsiness break something precious like a plate. *"Den peiraxi,"* I say, wanting to put them at ease. If it doesn't matter, what does—this bowl of beans that the daughter graciously serves? Oil is dripped in, the father pouring: a bit, more, then the whole grinning can. There on the roof by the piled firewood the three of us eat, while the overhead grapes melt into the reds of the uphill-stretching roofs.

Tiredness is a sail we are holding, as if by a cord at the end of our fingers. With it firm, all three of us climb in through a tiny dollbox window to stretch out on a floor's length of cloth and embroidered pillows.

Waking, I slip out through the window and down into the street. As I'm walking along the promontory above the cafes, gazing at the olive-necklaced hills of my walk to Aghiou Pareskevi, I hear the notes of a *serviko,* wild and grape and digit fast. Enchanted, I follow it up a snail-curl of streets to where on a ladder-reached trellised roof are gathered the men and band of the morning cafe. Who greet me with, "This is my Cloud Shoe father's roof, what can I do for you?" said in an Australian accent that here, among these white-sleeved, moustached presences doesn't seem quite so offensive. I point to the orchestra that has gathered round and say, "I like music— that fast Balkan *serviko* they were just playing."

"Oh," he says, brightening, "you dance then?"

"No, I just like music very much."

Unable to understand that a tourist can be his two quaffing eyes he persists, "But you must dance something—a twist, with me?"

Driven to the wall, I reply, "Twist, no, a *zembei-kiko,* maybe."

Whereupon a tall stork of man in old-fashioned ripply white sleeves and black vest asks if I will dance one with him. I accept, two or three glasses of ouzo are given me—downed in a tense silence—and the musicians strike up. My performance is what one might expect under the circumstances, a little too breathless, too full of odd disjointed slaps and leaps which leave me some minutes later, rather red-faced, while the musicians decide to call it an afternoon.

Behind them we file into the street where we reassemble, walking parade-style five abreast. Turning into a little street, we stop before a green house with an iron railing. While the musicians serenade, Cloud Shoes' wife comes out, bearing a silver tray adorned with glasses of ouzo that she will herself offer to each of us in turn. Since there are not quite enough glasses, you only touch mouth lightly to the rim, then reset it where the next can taste its opal brilliance. And the procession moves on, winding from one family doorway to another, before each of which messages must be poured into glasses, set afloat in our steaming hearts.

From the last we repair to Cloud Shoes' cafe, sitting now outside, on a ramp above the chests of the evening strollers. A lamb fresh from the spit is brought and choice morsels are placed in my mouth—fingers, forks, smiles.

We have reached the watermelon course when the Australian, who has been seated next to me translating, asks if I will draft him a "dying mother" letter to his consulate, requesting a year's visa extension. Surprised by the turn of events—this morning nothing would have seemed less likely—I go in with him to a corner table. When we return I feel like one of the family. I'm even offered a room for the night—but what about George?

The crowning accolade comes from Cloud Shoes, inviting me to dance a *zembeikiko*. From a man whose dancing so impressed me this morning, that's unrefusable. The bouzouki player looks up, nods, and at that moment my initiation begins. Try as I may, I cannot not dance. His great cloud of a belly holds me, gives me a moving background towards which I can direct the angles of my head, shoulders, feet, bringing them up just as close as I possibly can. A raft of glasses pours down on us, but, fearing to lose concentration, I postpone them until the piece ends.

What else do I dance? The intimacy suggests to him a *tsiftetelli,*

Cross your legs and think of what you'll do
Eat your mother's whiskers beat it in the blue

Lightness, a line of customers outside a Greek brothel on Saturday night? Gaiety that my head shakes with, my fingers whisper, as this woman's music plays, coiling me into its fine shadow-lace, its mounting, heaving clay.

I am there, a rose in sunset standing, while Cloud Shoes asks what else do I dance. Silence, I can't think of anything. But it would be impossible to go now, the floor would be so cold. As I hesitate, the orchestra on its own strikes up with a *serviko,* the very one that had brought me to their roof hours earlier. While Cloud Shoes stands to one side, clapping time, I, who have seen this two-step danced only once, do it by imagining my feet tied together like a horse. Hobbled thus, I hop until the sheer speed of the music has turned the blades of my feet into a pair of skates.

When I stop, unable to breathe, there comes an immense crescendo of offered glasses. Looking through their whites is like looking through smoke. Breathing them is like breathing mist. The last quaffed I return. To my table. To what the night still has in the other cafes to hold out: I wriggling on the floor, knees forward, neck thrust back, while over me Stork Clothes or George or the Local Idiot dances with an elegance, a power, that I help make happen. When at 3:30 a.m. the policeman blows his whistle there I am continuing on with a young kid to a rhythm provided by a cafe's two tables of women's and children's clapping hands.

The green field is stabbing me to a smile. The orange womb is looking up, higher. It may be dawn or it may be the end of the world, but I am sleeping.

Sleeves and music. Sleeves and music battering in my skull.

□

Waking, huge. Feeling quick sun, shadows. Drunkenly penetrated by white oblong shirts, smiles.

I put my shirt on and went out. Or rather, down a flight and sat. Then, back in the cafe, a yellow herbal liquid. Served in a tall glass with Melba toast and taking an hour to empty.

When I got outside it was to discover that the streets had during the night mysteriously fallen down. They lay on their backs, dishevelled, grinning, and occasionally a bit of blue or purple spit flowing off some near wall illuminated them. I took in these effects as cautiously as I was able to, toe, next toe, moving on points down down this embankment that yesterday had seemed street, that *kalamatiano's* sizzle of dark and spinning figures tracing their own deliberate dials over this now pocked and glass-like stone.

I sat down in Cloud Shoes' cafe and ordered an egg. Stared at it awhile, then upped the order to tomatoes. A full plate. Then walked, or rather curled my feet up the thirty feet of cobbles I had descended. Where there was my previously-ordered tea and everything was white square stone tables and mermaid and record singer calendars and pale fairy-tale blue walls.

Silence swam in and through the cafe and created something to which the edge of blue gave ship, a thing hulled in air; as much a part of the cliffside expanse as of the tin mugs and small-windowed terrace doors. Swam and changed the figures who came in and sat, a bouzouki in muted, siesta-observant hands, into so many relationships of space and glass. Their space, my glass. And the BLACK in and on that space means STAMP touching you crowbeards, dream turning far below in the urn soft silence.

Turning, touching, as in a wave, a good-bye, one into the other. Parapet wall along which once again I am walking, past faces riding up on brush-loaded donkeys, arms waving, and now towards last night's dancer a hearty recognition, "Panegyri, today still, why are you leaving?"

Out through the Magdalena gate like a spoon floating, the sloping stubble cut every now and then by the green fountain of a poplar, the blue gourd of a peasant shirt. Happiness, I think, is not the Simplon Express, not even with a glorious, hip-wagging, Barbara Stanwyck in it. It is something with strokes, hours, the perfect, because perforated, grass of song. Tall stick and I'm holding it. In my two liquid hands, my gigantic and moon-colored eyes.

☐

As always a last afternoon comes. I have intended to spend it walking in the Daphnis and Chloe valley below the town. As I go past the last of the cafes I hear a hiss, unmistakable. I enter and there, deep in a sprawl of glasses, are four very moustached faces. One lifts his ouzo and says, "Magdalena, I saw you dance, sit down!" while a second points to the black music case by the wall, meaning he is the town's bouzouki player, in eclipse since that evening shortly after arriving when I saw George and his cousin briefly dance.

There for one last afternoon we sit. The table is plain donkey gray. The chairs are rush. In them they are, as sunlight is. As this boy passing on muleback far below, deeply absorbed in tomorrow's toilet paper.

The waiter brings more ouzo, more white spots of cheese and plate and shirt. We catch it in our held, smiling, tugboat-banged glasses. *"As pethanei o thanatos,"*

("May death die!"), clinking toast after toast until the floor seems so many shards, the waiter not exactly smiling as he crouches amongst it, sweeping it up.

Around us a music develops, slow and enduring and calm; so calm you can't hear a wave break in these waters. Calm as trousers, as eyes, slits in a room where nothing is except coffee, except glass, except the reaching, exchanging slap-slap of card on table, against grin, by hair. The music is very lonely. It wants to be a horse in a stable, turning, stamping. But it can't sing and so sits there, buried in its glass.

Still you are just you, the devil come Johnny lately, wide-springing end to a bush of stars. Slur this in your teeth and, with shoulders out, start to get up, a little uncertainly. You are in the middle of the floor, a dropped cigarette curling you to a standstill. Stop, gather it, light it once more.

The bouzouki is now playing. Hands rough your skin. You are a boat sailing, about to. Voices call from the shore with offers of drinks. You pretend not to hear them. Your concentration is downwards: floor, shoe, well of your fit circling as you straighten up, smile, and plow on again. Around, around, the shore, the spilling stones. In the center of the floor is a soft pit. This on all accounts you must steer clear of, outlining with your hand its poised, pointed blue, but never entering it.

So you turn, widening arm until it makes a circle, a plunging boom. Widening and, in the effort, almost toppling over, and so coming to a stop, kneeling, as if beside yourself in grass. With a hand you plank down a star. The well comes out of the floor and barks. So big, you could almost put it between your arms and lift it. So big, you could almost say to it, "Feet, I've got them, let me use them to crush you, well." But never of course doing it. The pit must remain a pit, an evil center in a sparkling desert composed of these shirts, your friends, these spidery smiles more sensed than seen.

Glasses answer you, phosphorescent hair lingering with the tray presenting them, sign of the afternoon come back to. The table is there and around it once more like wet pieces of silver we sit, while the double-stringed music sweeps through one, then another table.

All very well for the start of a last ecstatic evening were there not George come to remind me of what I have forgotten, the farewell feast his family has prepared for us.

So off to that reeling home in the twilit lower village we go, where, among the morning-glories and the priceless view and the entire George family, is Betty. Fretting and letting me know that, no matter how many the dishes, she for one intends to be out by 9:30 p.m. to say her own farewells. Not, I would say, reckoning with a peasant feast. When a family tenders you one, you are meant never to rise from it. If you do, there are always the gifts, the embroidered table cloths and pillows which you must answer as best you can in cosmetics and nylon stockings and shaky promises to send more once back home. A feast isn't a feast, it's a lynching. Unable to do it cleanly by the rope and throat, they do the next best thing—make sure that when at 10:30 I do leave for the cafe, it is with my hands hooked around George and Strato's helping shoulders. There by me they sit (making sure no other family can get through) and next morning they are all at the Colonel's with smiles, waves of the hand, and baskets when the taxi arrives to take us away.

We are a few miles down the road when, looking down, I notice how black my hands are. From last night's dancing, Betty explains, all that sticky, smacked floor. With the memory there rises another; a man in a ten-foot circle of chairs and weathered faces spinning, his hands white drunken plates in a sea of viscous blues, reds. While beyond him, background against which the bouzouki's music breaks, turns, readdresses itself, the Turkish coast—blue like morning's skinny child, shyly, inseparably singing.

ZAMBIA

THE TRAVEL ITSELF BY LANDROVER through Northern and Luapula provinces I could probably have dispensed with. Bush is bush and in a world where any hundred yards was the same as the next hundred miles there was very little to look at. On the top of a dangerous, endlessly straight, gun-barrel road we drove, rarely meeting anything but an overturned truck or a pair of mallards quacking up from a pothole.

People were likewise few; four million in a country that by some estimates could hold fifty. In the villages the young men had gone away to work and we encountered only women and children and the old. Since the soil was poor and farming was of the semi-nomadic slash-and-burn variety there were no permanent houses. For centuries the people, a few warrior tribes aside, were cattle, traded from place to place as slaves. Unlike the West Africans, they did not seem to have systematic beliefs that related their sexuality to nature. The medicine man was someone you consulted only when all else had failed. Belief centered in the tribe, its hierarchies too fragile for the new coca-cola cash economy.

Fortunately I had a pair of binoculars. While my friend interviewed small village businessmen for a sociological study, I would wander about, using birds as a way of putting together a palette. Of course a traveller can find color anywhere. But in the streets of Italy or Iran it may seem more a matter of dress and buildings and park railings. It does not emanate from the forest pool of the skin. The African is color and that color is silence; so much so that a bit of jewelry takes on the vibrancy of a thrush call.

All this beckoned: women thin as a slice of water, mango smelling—a skin of drops on polished stone. Or a man's orange shirt that, in brightening the palm, made the muted rose-black of the forearm glisten. On a black person everything resonates, a total water where nose, temple, and chin appear and disappear in a single flash. Hands are stones, river is skin. Everything exists to take you down, make you soft: forest where the air is silver and only a pool somewhere bubbles and becomes breast, the two spots of the moonbathed sheet. Zambian beauty is a creation of curved lines modestly receding under tall conical hats and water-star earrings: pond-shadow eyes; the nose blunted, wide, a mountain projected in soft luminosity; turban-concealed hair, its pincurl partings forming rows like the streets of a thatch-hut village.

□

My trouble was not with the prostitutes, but the bars they invariably came with. The bar is the national institution; no one I spoke to had ever heard of one failing. Names like "Come to the City of Kitunsha Bar," (which says it all), "Stretch Your Legs," "Save Your Neck," "Don't Be Jealous," may suggest some of the varied attractions of these furnitureless, cement-floored, gym-sized bars with perhaps a raised corner platform set off with mirrors where men and women separately flash.

The violence comes from the bowling pins of beer, the whole of which must obviously be drunk. Beer is the one drink a bar serves and comes only in that size, or even larger Congo-smuggled bottles. Recently I read where President Kuanda, the founder of Zambia, threatened to resign rather than preside over a nation of drunkards. If you ask a Zambian why he goes to a bar, he will probably answer, "To joke." Much of this joking is traditional; so, if a member of the leopard clan reaches into your "rat" trousers and gooses you by way of greeting, nothing need be amiss. It's his prerogative and you must have others.

But in the new towns such gestures may give rise to a scuffle.

This fighting is so feared that often proprietors have two bars side by side: one for fighting, and one more polite with female company: high-school girls on vacation, divorced tribal princesses, mothers with diaperless babies like health certificates on their backs.

These waitresses, bar-girls, whatever, are called prostitutes. All the term means is that they don't belong to anyone and aren't local. I never knew one not to accept whatever I had laid out and our interpreter had two personal rules: never pay, and never say when you are leaving town.

With such casualness, and no common language, there can be misunderstandings. I remember one long tense walk under a full moon back to my hotel in which the girl and I were followed by two men who had been waiting for her to finish work. The men, one of whom was a cousin, the other a fishmonger, kept insulting her, and now and then would come up to try to shoulder us off the road and into the ditch. She kept trying to reassure me, "Don't be afraid," the one phrase she seemed to possess, before launching into "One Zambia, one nation." But this plea for interracial tolerance was clearly falling on deaf ears. As we turned up a long hill the pace got much brisker. We were near the top when she suddenly bolted in the direction of a single-bulb-lit building. This turned out to be the local police station. So there we found ourselves, cadging matches, giving our various ages and occupations—to our giggle of disbelief the fishmonger, a young-looking man, gave his age as forty—while the girl, in that quiet African way, explained how she was being hassled. Finally, after some forty-five minutes, with the policeman leading the way, we set off on a tow path to my hotel. While the men conferred on the porch, the girl once again bolted to lock herself in my room.

To make love in such conditions might seem ideal. But the emotional advantages don't always compensate for the beer you have had to drink while outwaiting everyone else and which turns any lovemaking into the progress of a salmon gasping his way up over waterfalls. Not that the girl hasn't been well-coached. And for sheer willingness in reviving a limp penis she can't have very many Western equals. She raises her knees until they are up over your shoulders. She makes the vagina lips press out like an elephant trunk. Before you know it, you are sucked in, not knowing by what right all this is being done, but willing enough to accept the hardening miracle.

But this percussion culture with the shoulder-propped legs and the vagina cavity compressed to its drumlike maximum can make you feel as if you are being stretched out on an interminable railroad track: no rotation, just bang, puff, smoke, steam. There until morning's fire lights the skies the two of you contend, trying to score as many leaping hits off her back wall's bullseye as the beer allows.

Things needn't be so rushed. As with any stranger there is a tension to be gotten rid of. So time may go by sitting on a park bench, her legs straddling yours, until the warmth of the trust, the mutual exoticism, can begin welling up. To put you at your ease she may start asking questions, "Are you married?" "Do you have children?" Not to be out done, you ask her about hers (all prostitutes have them). Soon other points intrude. Neither of you is exactly a native here.

So the two of you in the most limited English converse, she perhaps showing you some of the vicissitudes of her trade, the bite marks, the broken incisor, until she feels free enough to lean back, offering you her breasts to fondle. It is the final assurance she needs and it will carry her through the warren of mud passageways, not to your room, but hers: a gay pecking on a pane by way of a knock; a rattling of chains and you are in with sister and baby, you a large foreign dope standing in the corridor, knowing by what right the place is yours, but feeling little sexual interest in your beer-depressed body.

To give yourself time, step with your penis out into the courtyard's lake of mud, knowing that the whole sullying sequence of splashes must ring in tenement ears like the rudest of phone awakenings.

Meanwhile, arrangements are proceeding. Places for the spectators must be found. Theatrically, a red curtain material is floated across the head of the bed leaving a passageway to one side. She has already peeled off her nightclub clothes and is in a white slip; what she wears, she explains, for those whom her large body might offend—those like you! It is also a sign of what remains withheld, like those surprisingly sweet kisses she now and then favors you with.

While I play with her stockings she starts grilling me. The one thing she requires in a man, she announces, is someone who won't evade. (But if I didn't want to evade, I wouldn't be here, in this country, sitting gloomily faced by these sheets. Isn't my whole personality based on just such a surreptitious folding out, a dance into not exactly meaning?) I am pondering this when she asks, "Why didn't you dance at the club, don't you like to?"

A bit miffed I answer, "I like some dances very much, but rock isn't me."

"What do you dance then, show me!" For a confounded instant in the little passageway I comply, miming a zembeikiko. Unable to continue under their scrutiny I slump down on the bed, feeling this beats most anything in pre-bed rigamarole.

Appeased, she tells me her opinion, "A *gege* man," and calling, asks her sister for confirmation. So the two inspect me sitting on the edge of the bed in my shorts. "What is *gege*?" I ask. As the two dissolve in giggles, I begin to suspect it means the sort of guy who comes on as a child, sword lost in the stone.

Now that I know the worst she turns off the light; I roll into bed first, and there things are unaccountably warm, even passionate, and as such, incomprehensible. So from sword to star I rise, sucked up by pleasure, not knowing anything and not wishing to: because self-knowledge, whatever the long term results, pulls me up short, stuttering on the ice? Because I'd rather live and breathe by obsession, "I need this, therefore I'm here," this being the offered heavy-lipped sweetness, these hips that I dig my nails into, rise along, a kingfisher poised in air, rattling his colors.

Coming a second time is like trying to climb a mountain, all that I haven't as yet pissed out. But such is the effect of sunrise, its new fresh snow, that I almost succeed in the enormity of my task before slipping back down. So, sleep, heads on the one shared, soft pillow, faces turned away from each other like brothers.

After waking and leaving enough to explain my absence, I slip out past all these signs that I must remember and down to my hotel where I wash up. Then out to a cafe, empty except for two thin girls chatting at a near table. Watching them I realize what I should do. So I buy some breakfast rolls and, with a shirt and a spare wallet, return to the cabin. From now on everything is extra, these photographs that they show me, this sex for which in full view I must climb in bed, she squatting in her favorite position above. As a final treat I am offered her daughter's six-year-old crotch to kiss, "A local custom," she calls it.

It is my last couple of hours, but perfectly at home now I sit watching the room brightening behind the curtain's sun red, or baby-sit the daughter in the mud yard, warding off her efforts to inspect the burnt stick of my penis. The world has become wild again.

MADAGASCAR

THERE ARE ANY NUMBER OF REASONS why, on a trip to East Africa, one might choose to cross over to this large, red, eighteen-tribe island located some hundred and fifty miles out in the Indian Ocean. Mine went back to a dream about lorises I had in 1968 at the time of the civil rights disturbances on the Berkeley campus.

I had first become aware of lorises through a friend's physical anthropology course. But the animals of my dream were not, in point of fact, lorises, but lemurs, a long-tailed, inquisitively-eyed fellow prosimian that the great depth of the African channel has preserved until recently from monkey competition. In Madagascar there are some twenty-three species of lemur (all more or less endangered). Those of my dream had the long black torso and short toothpick arms that I associate with Willie McCovey, the long-time Giant first baseman.

In dreams mistakes are crucial and it was perhaps inevitable that a punster in my private dream machinery should have seized upon "loris." If I found lorises so beguiling, what about the Loire, the river of castles, poets, and the purest spoken French? In a jiffy here I was being set down in the very center of all that I had studied and yearned after: willow trees, crystal-green water, low grassy banks, here and there a fisherman's rowboat. If it had set up a whole exquisite picnic table I would not have been at all surprised. But something new, a sense perhaps of where my real loyalties lay, managed to resist these blandishments and instead switched the dream back to lorises and their dense, coppery-leaved Madagascar jungle. They were my brothers and from their verge of extinction were crying out for recognition.

All this took time to realize and may have been meant to, since the dream explained my reluctance to throw in my lot with the Black Power movement which

had resulted, for one, in our English department's
firebomb-gutted Wheeler Hall. Instead I believed that a
humanity worth fighting for had to embrace not only
Blacks, but the whole evolutionary chain back to lemurs
and shrews.

This may sound like some clever counter-revolu-
tionary ploy. But there may be more to dreams and the
way they prepare you for your future than that. For it was
during these three weeks in Madagascar that I was to get
my first glimpse of a communally responsible society.

My first impressions did not augur well. You do
not expect to be greeted at Tananarive airport by a bat-
talion of jungle-clad, crew-cut, tommy-gun waving
French paratroopers. They had been called in by the government to help put down a tribal revolt in the far south-
west. (Later I was to hear a captured chieftain say that the
last thing he or his tribe wanted was to fight the republic's
government. But when you are starving what else can you
do to call attention to your plight?)

The countryside I found myself in was plateau,
hill-encircled and in mid-April now rather chilly. Only
this was a wet plateau, cut into tiny pond-plots; each with
its man in it, often up to his hatted, blue-shirted neck in
the mud, he and the bullock, or some twenty fully-clothed
women. On a raised dike of sorts the road wound, past
houses of orange brick with maroon or brown-painted
balconies, very tall and thin like those a child might draw.

To this Indonesian Africa was to be added the
French exoticism of downtown Tananarive with its hordes
of stalled, honking, *quatre chevaux*, its cafe awnings and
soccer posters. On a vast traffic island, across from the
restaurants and French hotels, flared the white umbrellas
of the Friday market or *zoma*, said to be the world's
largest.

Compounding my isolation was the dose of clap I
had contracted on my last stop on the island of Lamu. I

am not sure what I did that first afternoon. I probably spent it slowly walking around the market fringes, depressed by the Asiatic misery, the ladies who sat all day on a stairway nursing four piles of nuts (constantly rearranging them, moving them up into a better light), or three oranges, or just a pair of children and an upturned hat.

The second day I decided to take in a soccer game between the national team and Malawi. The stadium lay, cupped like a lake, at the bottom of a crater. The roofs and staircases surrounding it were such that you had no need to buy a ticket to see the game. And those Seurat dots with their conical straw hats sitting on the stone steps that led up to the queen's palace may well have outnumbered the thirty thousand of us inside.

The game itself was more of a pitched battle than a game, perhaps because the substituted referee, a Malawi official, did not dare exercise control. But the storm on the field hardly took precedence over the one we made. In the course of three hours, not twenty feet from me, two men died of heart attacks. After the game, the losing Malawi team had its bus stoned. At one point the field became entirely covered in expensive oranges and the players went around, glad for the moment's respite in the heat, picking them up and punting them back into the stands.

On the third day, a Monday, I visited the hotel doctor. He confirmed the gonorrhea, prescribing a drug that turned my urine purple, while forbidding any alcohol, pimento, or sex for a week. There was also a course of four daily injections.

This regime with its noon injection—two quick slaps on the butt to make me relax and in with the needle—helped me settle down. It is hard to go far when you only have half a day. Soon I began to appreciate Tananarive. Not that this was hard; during my stay I never heard anyone speak badly of the city, a fact that in our world speaks volumes. For one, there are almost no policemen; one hundred in the whole of the city. Sidewalks are glassless, and not disfigured by dogs. If the downtown is a shrieking crater, the hills offer a quick escape. Once up by one or another staircase, you enter a residential silence of arched churches and gay, maroon-balconied, orange brick houses too steep for car or shop.

Here prostitutes announced themselves with a friendly, "Etes-vous bien?" or to show their availability would start gaily singing. The local art is raffia-weaving and there are baskets for everything: books, groceries; also baskets for the head, inverted, with a pair of strings or a ribbon around it. The most hatted are the children, sign of oriental vulnerability to what by African standards is a mild sun.

I came to admire the market vendors perched on crates in front of their little piles of bananas and bitter oranges, each pile so delicate that one thinks of a collection of marbles. Much of the rest of Tananarive had that same child-colored air: the orange and maroon somehow creating between them, as their roofs rise against the hillside, that space slanted in shadow with which the Merinian sets off himself; his black streaming hair, his eyes like yellow glinting suns staring out of their dark skin from a doorway.

Compared to the African with her thin stilt-like legs that go on being legs until like a flower they disappear in the vase of the waist, the Western woman sticks out, a cubist collection of whistle-stops, figure-eights... The Malgache is cubist too; but hers is a round cubism like those *rovas*, hilltop burial mounds that look out on a landscape of volcanic circles. And, like a volcano, there is a feeling of waiting explosivity which somehow contrives to remain soft, soft as clay, fingernail indentable, little ripples pouring forth from all its salient points. And the face is at one with it, a sort of potato, but with a freshness that transforms the rest of the body, lends it mist. Hats have the effect of haloing the naturally oval contours, accenting the yellow-brown and making it shine with its own straw light. The hat, as worn by the women, can also be a mask; or it is replaced by parasols of sombre butterfly-like elegance. Under it comes a sort of gunman's scarf, or the traditional white *lamda* shawl falling like a scallop shell over the back.

Each afternoon, in respect to my dream, I would take a bus out to the botanical garden where the lemurs had their zoo. For hours I would stand watching them as they hopped about with their large, erect, feathery tails and vaulted over one another, or sat large-eyed in their barbed-wire preserve, patiently grooming each other. If I had a personal coat of arms they would be there, green on a leaping branch-sea.

I hadn't yet spoken to a native when, on my fourth day, as I huddled between two buildings during a brief squall, I found myself accosted by an out-of-work road engineer. My telling him of the record he had just broken seemed to inspire him, for he promptly invited me up to his house. He was in town to see his uncle, a radio official, about a loan so that he could buy his baby a tin of similac.

There to the radio station we went, to learn that the uncle had been left cash-short by a recent operation. I volunteered what was needed. With the tin triumphantly between us, we staggered up to his house set in the rear of a small courtyard with a separate kitchen giving a spectacular view of the whole city.

Having wormed my way into their home I was not about to let their lack of money stand in the way of the meal that in other circumstances they would have given me. If they had no food, I could buy all five of us a meal for less than it would cost me to eat alone and badly in a restaurant. These arguments carried the day. Back down the enormous staircase we went to borrow a red table cloth and purchase the needed ingredients.

Despite the hazards of the courtyard in the dark—the main meal must have been lunch—a red and orange town-colored meal was produced: a salad of grated carrots sprinkled with lemon, followed by a broth of ginger-flavored vermicelli, with the remains of the broth being used to cook the main dish of rice. My friend did the cooking himself. Merinian men, he explained, are naturally domestic, giving the children their bath and sharing in all the housework except washing and ironing. My host had too much pride to invite me for a second meal as he had promised, much as I looked forward to it. But my tongue had been set loose and next day, while poking around the vacation-closed university, I asked a student if he could recommend a hotel—a native hotel. In a way that was to become typical, not only did he give me the name of one, but he personally escorted me there.

From the start I enjoyed my hotel with its Vietnamese restaurant and popular bar. The room itself with its vast lopsided bed I occupied almost stealthily. There were commodes, but I never used them, preferring to spread my things out in a heap on the floor. What thief would want to rummage through a slag pile? Soon I was acquiring new material for it and even reading there, my goods functioning as bolsters.

Out in the streets I became this large white foreign oaf again, arms pawing like one blind. But nothing seemed to get in the way, the streets opening like cataracts through which I stumbled, emitting my own dragon smoke. To be so large and so stupid, I could see these lithe Merinians drawing a smug comfort from that. Yet I'd keep on being my eyes, this head on a long-necked pole peering into the recesses. Everywhere this nervousness flickered around me. I couldn't walk, I couldn't sit down. Therefore gardens, a chance to put my knees up on a bench and experience the peace that not being all-surrounded brings.

Here a notebook and pen became what wiper-blades are to a car. Whereas a book only half-absorbed. At the end of a page I'd be on my feet frantically search-ing myself, wondering what I had mislaid.

Better yet a wood. Here only the ears existed, feeling their way forward in the dark like mice. So all those wretched Saturday symphony mornings hadn't been wasted, I'd think, buoyed by a recurring past. And when supper at my hotel came, it found me museful, ready to be myself among others. These were the moments to discov-er how the eye noted each new arrival as a splashing for-ward in the dust toward a waiting bowl and chair. A water glass, a napkin in a bowl, a mahogany crocodile ashtray, these calmed the eyes even before the bowl of hot water with its sprig of watercress, or a few grape leaves, arrived. And I'd look around, noting the butterfly-folded napkins, the abstract incised design on an ebony grandfather clock, the four corner panels of a grisaille-painted night still-ness, houses and empty courtyards as seen by a returning spirit.

The hotel gave me a passport. I had only to men-tion where I was staying for invitations to extend. And these chance acquaintances would actually turn up a fort-night later; to take me to a Sunday cock fight, or to the popular theater, a few steps from the slum dwelling where my host, a French-educated ceramics professor whom I had met at an early morning bus stop, had been born. It was at this theater that I understood for the first time what a communally responsible art might involve.

Imagine a market-shaped building with an open roof, white and lilac walls, a few tiny paintings for decora-tion along with a sign, "Don't spit on the walls." The re-mainder is taken up by the stage floor, hung with pennants, big enough to accommodate a troup of fifteen actor-singers. Around it on tiered benches the populace sits, spitting out their oranges and talking to one another. Unlike a Western audience, they do not lean back and quietly smirk. No, they participate fully, yelling encouragement to an accompaniment of tossed coins, shrieks, and dove-like moans.

The rear of the stage is draped in an orange cloth, and of the two competing troups one is likewise in orange dress with black-banded straw hats and long flowered shawls flung over the shoulder. During the whole of the performance the musicians will keep their hats on, whereas the actors leave them in a circle in the middle of the floor. Directing from a scorebook is the local Verdi, an old man in a royal blue uniform, bemedalled like a hotel doorway. The troup are peasants from one of the twelve surrounding hills. And they are not ashamed to proclaim it, "As you know the rice harvest is on. If we trip up, it's because we haven't had time to practice properly." The Malgache is constantly telling you his shortcomings; not out of masochism, but because like an athlete he knows that his moment has yet to come. By the same token there is nothing that can't be put off. One would think there is nothing more final than death. At one moment, our friend is with us. At the next, he is in his box, gone forever. And it is this that provokes all those hysterical scenes, the women throwing themselves weeping onto his coffin, or jumping into his pyre. In Madagascar a man is buried. Fine, that's all right, we'll be seeing him later. And a year later, at a time when the stench isn't quite so bad, they all assemble on the hillside where he has been entombed for a great party in which they take him out of his box and, one by one, dance with him.

A shifting box of colors best describes the impression made by this deep, fifteen person chorus. Everything is performed in unison, but there is always somebody new standing in front of you, holding up the palm of a hand, lifting an eyebrow. And singing, singing so strongly that you wonder how he manages to stay in one piece.

The material comes from the same sort of uplifting tripe that Sa'adi collected in the Gulistan, i.e. the tale of the "Honest Orphan." But the unison gives the tale the strength of a mass affirmation, a truth that one actor and then another successively embodies. And the performers don't hold themselves above the audience with some such drivel like we're artists. No, they are just like us, all the more because of their weird orange, nineteenth-century frock coats. What is more democratic than the past? And it is the voice of the ancestors that delivers the homilies with such sincerity, such black-soled feet and gold-toothed grins. Gripping by what is common, the performance distills a marvelous fraternity: we live, we are one, we can be good. Imagine fifteen voices shouting that, punctuated by huzzahs!

I have seen the two competing troups both perform when a kid I have met at a bus stop comes up to me, a fighting cock under his arm. Off we go, for fifteen minutes following a track made for small, shoeless feet through the rice fields. His cock, he says, is small, but very brave, undefeated in six fights. On the way, to make conversation, I ask about the scars all down both arms. "Made by roosters?" I ask, naively, "No," he says, "Malgache women."

Compared to that sort of blood fest a cock fight may seem rather tame. Ours takes place in an abandoned rice field, the tiny rise of the dike forming a viewing area where the men squat, the children just a little ahead. Behind them a ways are women with carts of food. A compote-sized potato salad, served like a curry, with tomatoes, carrots, herbs, and greens all floating about in water, will cost a penny.

The pairing off—like any fight a matter of size—takes place with the handlers all grouped together in an oval ring. Then comes the placing of bets. The fight, punctuated by respites for dashes of water (over crest and feet) ends when one of the cocks turns tail, something the cock is extremely reluctant to do since at that moment he enters the family stew. But how passionately the audience enters into it, each rise in the air, and practically each peck, eliciting Flamenco-like shouts, exclamations, or moans of disappointment.

Rice requires an intensive cultivation. You don't burn down the bush and throw out some seed and call it a day. That same intensity radiates all the way through Malgache life. Everywhere you look there are people running. The ricksha drivers, or the pair of boys with a great side of beef slung between them on a pole, you might be prepared to discount. But not the waiters hurtling out of their kitchens, tray in hand with that look of a sprinter coming out of his blocks. Garbage men lope alongside their truck, and even little girls, normally the most sedate of creatures, play between the curbs a game of grasshopper leaps and much wild scurrying which is to hopscotch what badminton is to tennis.

□

In some countries a bus ride into the hills of the Betsileo country would be a matter of some trepidation. Here it was more like a festival. The steps creating the community might seem but the most halting. Perhaps someone from under his jacket produces a bag of peanuts, or a peeled orange, and silently offers it. Or an old man with a ravaged (syphilitic?) face taps me to everyone's embarrassment on the shoulder to ask why he can't have any children. There are eight rows of us all crunched to-gether like olives in a jar. But should a passenger pop up on the roadside everyone grins and squeezes over. Maybe a man in the rear starts singing. Or we run into a down-pour so that the side flaps have to be lowered, blotting out any view. Or we pull up in the middle of nowhere, by a small river: for a piss, a stretch? No, so the women can get out, every single last one of them, and, standing in it up to their waists, wash themselves and their underpants. Little things, but they all mount up, and such is the mo-mentum that, even after you have arrived, you keep being accosted by fellow passengers only too pleased to be able to invite you to something, a bar, a movie, a block's stroll.

This hospitality is not confined to those with whom you have shared something like a bus trip. In the hill towns I could not go for a walk without having some countryman leap out of the bush to offer me something: a cake, a couple of hard-boiled eggs, some freshly-roasted peanuts. The Malgache can do this with intrepidity be-cause he has no fear of your refusing him. One can see in this a sign of their oriental deviousness, like the Eskimo who gives and gives (a dog, his wife) for the pleasure of watching you lose face. Perhaps. But it may also be a way of expressing trust, of saying one is not afraid.

As one goes south the Merinian's white robes give way to something pink or apricot-colored. A hat for the sun. This hat radiates, a great globe glistening with friendliness. The rest of his garments are a series of over-hanging shelves. Under the robe something woolen that hangs down to the knees, collared and buttoned and sleeved to look like a shirt. Maybe under it something white and frayed and a black coat. People still grow rice, but cattle now dominate, long-horned, hump-backed, black-and-white zebus. Houses seem to have more fan-tasy, more orange or red flame in them, with bits of func-tional design stuck onto the outside in the form of a ladder, or outside staircase. The rolling alternation of hills and rice fields with their constant surprises of bluff, of house, give way to a thin line of mountains, no longer something irrigable, but pure stagecraft.

The markets are hard to catch as they happen but once a week. When I would arrive it would be too late usually for anything but a glimpse of some promenading, bare-chested, teenage accordionists, or an old hatted man with both feet dreamily dribbling an orange through the straw refuse. All the same, I could feel an elation which wasn't just the straw on the ground and the buses and people rolling up sacks of unsold grain and the robed men with their umbrellas hooked into the backs of their shirts belting down red rum in the bars.

The final scene, the row of herdsmen in their glinting hats and sunset-tinged robes sitting with their long wavering crooks against a background of poinsettia trees and cayenne-red earth, is something impossible to convey. One thinks by comparison of Africa. Only there the colors take on a round, darting butterfly-like movement; whereas on the Madagascar plateau the colors, variegated as they are, remain finally static, as, say, the panels of a rose window are static.

There really isn't motion: just that every time you open your eyes the whole kaleidoscope has shifted, rearranged itself. And the elements are so varied—the girl dressed in a beautiful modern discord of orange and pink, dress and parasol; the men in their overhanging shelves of robe, wool shirt, under-jacket—it's hard to know what to aim your pen at first.

A TREK IN NEPAL

OF ANY HOLY PLACE WE ASK THAT IT give us a ground to dance on: with our feet, if we can; if not, with our eyes, plunging them where we can't otherwise reach—into submission, charity.

To arrive for the first time in the streets of Katmandu is visually bewildering. Has one ever seen fire-and-lightning caps before, a green door, a spinning wind? Colors race about, turning each street into a virtual fountain.

Perhaps one has caught something of this in the riot of a spring meadow, the bird-and-leaf flash of a fall road. Only here the phantasmagoria is people: blue people, green people, red people, orange people; more flash of canes, necklaces, caps, belts, bangled arms and feet than in the most eye-popping Persian bazaar. Each is his moment, his bright swinging eyes in his red-beaded calm, standing by a construction project, or putting out his cigarette in a hotel lobby. To struggle alone under great bags of cement cannot be much fun. To do it while surrounded by sitting comrades, each clearly a spoke of light, may well be a consolation.

If by Western standards Nepal seems very happy, it also ranks among the world's poorer societies. One can see why in the fifties the governing autocracy might have chosen to reverse its former policy of exclusion and welcome the hard currency we tourists brought in, useful in purchasing salt, medicines, fuel and other essentials. As observers, too, we may have had our use. At a time when across the border in Tibet the world's greatest theocracy was being summarily erased, Nepal needed all the live testimony she could muster to assert that she wasn't another Shangri-La.

The catch was us tourists. Our wants may not have seemed that harmful: a topfloor apartment among the old city's knobbed and curling pagoda roofs from where tea could be served to a few friends. Now even here the views pale before the blare of the taxis. Introduced to hie us back and forth from the airport, they have multiplied to where Katmandu is one endless honking din. These taxis, in turn, have their own needs—oil, asphalt, perhaps a house for the driver in the former ricefields— with the result that the ring of surrounding mountains remains for months on end but sensed presences.

If I can't avoid the pollution, I can rise above some of it by hiring a bicycle. Suspended in a cooler air, I join a gliding, giraffe-like throng that leaves me free to peer over the compound gardens, while checking out the sidewalks: Thamangs in baggy, pita-bread colored garments, set off by a black vest and lightning-flash cap; Newar women like hibiscus-hued katydids as they shuffle along in their gauze transparencies, all woven mountain mist and red-camellia-plaited hair.

Other sights conform more to legend: the great, ear-flapping, cloud-swift stride of an elephant; or a man alone in the river gravel, with brush and a bar of soap swabbing down a water buffalo.

□

Better still if you go for a walk at dawn. First, a pink, smoky suffusion. This rapidly gives way to a great pumpkin sun shining through a cold haze in which each sound hangs as if sculpted.

By the roadside women appear, rose-kindled, blue-gathered, stooped to their ablutions. While down it small barefoot Thamangs scurry past, bent double under a load of leaves and faggots—the second-hands of destruction.

Beyond the city the rice terraces fan out in steep, curve-bladed rivulets, their lime brilliance set off by a plot of mustard or potatoes. But no path or border to the houses, which seem to rise helter-skelter, flowers occurring on an upstairs ledge, pink against a bedroom's oblation bowls and religious pictures.

Farmhouses, too, are tiered in a wash of cinnamon over yellow, leaving the thatch of the sharply-pitched roofs to make them one with the surrounding green. More lovely still the way, above the bare threshing floor and animal-hitching posts, the pronged upper story swells, more vase than house, more sky than door.

Everywhere the floating ships of the temples. They are the people's songs, drifting up to the honored, dragon-cloud sky. Coming upon them I feel carved, as if I were myself a block of wood. Sitting, my lips, parted, ring doors open, a room's waterbowl in whose depths blossoms float and mosquitoes dwindle away into prayer: "All my leaves liquid upfloating to you, maker of these skies, so queasy light."

☐

It's the religious architecture for which the valley is justly famous. For women there is the shrine represented by the vast statue of the serpent-ringed Vishnu asleep on a leaf of the cosmic ocean that I came upon in an open-walled pool. If terrestrial life is, as Hindus believe, Vishnu's dream creation, then our survival may be a matter of keeping him from ever waking up. But in this thin-aired, tropical climate, with the midday sun blasting down on that enormous, exposed, black body, even the most creative of sleepers may start to toss and turn. Hence these anointings that the women bring, sprinkling petalled water out of little breast-size teapots, or with their own lips stooping to kiss the great turmeric-and-nasturtium-wreathed feet.

For us men, while awaiting the enlightenment that will allow us too to be Vishnu, there are the kindred satisfactions offered by the Buddhist pagodas of Patan.

First, a series of terraces. These may have no other point than to get you used to the idea of being there, prostrate, hands pointed forward, touching, drumming, beating. Seven flights up, adrift in a cry of white flashing pennants, is a gold crown. The whole open-sided in-between is a tossing, totally hypnotic dance of levels: swaying orifices; swelling plenitude. Birds fly in and out, long-tailed monkeys scamper about, from the beam supports a girdle of dangling gold leaves and carved dog bodies juts, inviting you to add your own to the monstrous pile. All this squatting, sway-backed feminine splendor is capped by a red-and-gold roof from the top of which a face-like gong glows amid white pennants. Then, rising out of the gong, a flashing *dorje* sceptre.

It is perhaps the hope that this sceptre can be mine that impels me, lying on my back, to send my eyes higher than they have ever strained. I see the top roof agleam with golden nodules that quiver with each shake and toss of my head. As I rattle them I see the pagoda itself becoming more rotund, more femininely squat-like. A bell twanged, a lidded prayer cask rotated, what matter! Or all matters because I now see the sky, this home, as the answer to my hands, this rushing, river-white breathing, being pulled up, made more round, more eternal. "At the entrance to everything, I Vishnu, shall instill the world." What each of us suppliants thinks, dreaming through stone lids of the nasturtium paste gilding the naked, sky-open temple of our body. Around the head the raft of cobra hoods, tongues uplifted, wanting more, more fire, more sky. To be roasted, sucked up, delivered unto.

Like night, rose-water, hands, all that she brings, is: these dove-spotted breasts into whose lavender I sink as into that avenue all sunken shadow and column-lined in that mysterious kingdom beneath the waves. I am darker, my temples glow with a whole ringing forest of song that takes me to her bed, there to girt me in these roses with which her lips now usher me out, day-broken, smiling.

On the eve of the trek, thinking of those mountains where Terror will shortly ride his wheels over me I am still. Lost for many seconds I am still. If my hands flutter like prayer flags, my tongue doesn't follow. Absorbed, all is absorbed: moon, fishes, and this godsent earth. All this dreams. It has never been and neither have I, I think, looking at what across the temple road sits similarly entranced. Oh, for a word of light to breathe motion into those massive stone curlicues! Far from that, my sandals breathe, contained rather than radiating. I would like to put on my fisherman's gown, dance with Shiva's eyes into nonentity, flame. But I can't, any more than I can lift my eyes to what is within me, growing. Instead I must quietly tilt back my head, hope another day's radiance finds me once more within it.

☐

These fears might seem exaggerated. All I was going on was a walk, not some perilous clinging to a rock ledge. But walks in the Himalayas inevitably carry a spiritual tinge and these mountains were of an unrelinquishing grandeur; every time I lifted my eyes I felt exalted. Yet the walking itself was painful, the result of a knee cartilage I had unknowingly torn a few months earlier.

The knee might not have acted up without the sneaker-boot combination I affected after the first day. I had taken a wrong turn at virtually the first tree fork. By the time I had caught them up the hurrying in boots that weren't well enough broken in had blistered one of my heels.

In the circumstances it made sense of a sort to combine a sneaker with a boot. While the one probed, the turtle-like other could smash fearlessly ahead. Between them I felt proof to most eventualities.

But I hadn't reckoned on what the difference would do to my spine, since the sneaker had to proceed on tiptoe to keep abreast of its giant companion. Eventually my knee began to react to all these unwarranted assumptions, this great sixty-person-strong expeditionary force. That may have been what got me lost: wanting to put as much space as possible between myself and this barefoot, tubercular-grunting mob, each with some 120 pounds of gear strapped to his forehead. After a sharp climb in the border sun this was more than I could bear. So I lit out, hoping to note a few birds.

This bolt, which necessitated a Sherpa being dispatched to find me, was my last. By the time we had caught them up he had dinned into me the difference between a private stroll and a trek in which one is doing twenty miles a day in order to cross Tesi Lapcha before the monsoons.

With the loss of freedom came a new sense of purpose measured by how one kept pounding along. The porters did it superbly, whereas I, despite regular soccer, was clearly in trouble. Everything bespoke a zenith: the pass, the campsite towards which I was striving. In that sustaining purpose I walked, envious of these human chimes so cheerfully serene, their faces even when bowed reflecting their pleasure in being part of this vast circulation of light, wind, river, and stones.

I am speaking with an exaggeration that may only denote the half hour late that I daily limped in. For others progress may have been less illuminating, this will I or won't I tapped on every rock face. But I suspect what I felt was abnormal only in its hobbling intensity. The signs of the evil to be warded off were everywhere: in the inscribed *mani* stones; in the consideration of a promontory's slate-engraved seats; a hard, bright-green leaf holding out all of a hillside's trickle like a hand. In a world where all activity is regarded as spiritually endangering we human trucks need all the stop, look and listen signs we can get. So, when in the middle of a path a *mani* stone appears take it, British style, on your right. And mutter something, *"Om mani padme hum,"* (May the Jewel Blast in your Name, Lord, ever more!).

□

If the walking was hard, the mornings were signally beautiful. Bright knocks to blue kingdoms "make mountains!" I'd cry, astonished at these apparitions that seemed cut out of cardboard; in blue sky a white tub of leaping ink. Walking, I'd feel all contained, as if I were on the base of a great pot. "That tree," I'd note, "is on my left and the light cuts it like a swooping hawk." Two hours later I'd be hard pressed to tell one tree from another. Everything had become this crashing glittering in which each shale flake struck its paranoiac note.

Why not stop, sit down for a moment, and relax. How else remember?

By thinking about it, thinking that "train in the night," this ever-stretching, receding human chain swinging me by one foot, now the other, as if from bank to bank. "Nothing is around me," I'd tell myself, trying to concentrate. Should a forager appear at a bend of the road, eyes welling forth in a greeting, I kept walking. In a landscape of stone the trekker becomes one himself, concerned only with stepping over, around, by them.

Finally a moment came when I had to sit down, busy myself with my thermos; less for the water than the respite that the rucksack provided. "I am reaching to the head of the stair," I'd find myself mumbling, back on my feet, "I have nowhere to go—but up."

Around me wind circled a dry desperation. Maybe some red-beaked choughs ash-floated by. Or a red beetle appeared at lap height, not far from a patch of orange moss. Everything else shrank to the modicums of breath, this knowing I must once again stop, find my eyes some shadowy crevice in which to tunnel.

My exasperation focused on the dearth of presence. But where mountains absorb so much, what else can thrive? Better to feel their grave stilts pressing me down where Sherpa and moss live with beetle and star and the yak pastures in what must be the cleanest of earthly sties.

□

Much of this rancor would vanish with lunch, invariably celebrated under trees, by a clanging, sun-lidded stream. Afterwards legs felt like good stout planks again, ready to walk wherever the chain should take me. "More upgoing, downgoing," a kitchen porter teased as he prepared to dash on ahead, to have tea ready when we arrived.

"Stop-going," I felt like replying, irked by the lack of levelness in these valley-straddling paths.

Then the first breezes would begin to stir, chest-high cornstalks waved their terraced green where I prodded myself down, along, in the rising fastness of the late shadows.

Where everything comes from up to down, down to up, there is no reason not to be slow, white hat on head, teeth glittering in the chastening wind.

□

A constant mystery as we picked from one valley to the next were the steps hewn in the rock face. How, or by whom this was done I can't imagine, for I never saw a man, hatchet in hand, on a path. Most of those we passed were foragers, usually boys and girls in their late teens. There was one such party who for the whole of an afternoon walked beside a friend and I. Every now and then they would make us stop and proffer a match. One had a harmonica, the others their lips and mouths. They kept insisting that we dance for them. On a rain and wind-washed promontory we obliged, shifting scarves to a belly dance-like two step. Then they picked up their round barrows and hastened on. At each succeeding viewpoint there they would be, ranged in a circle with their harmonica, waiting. This passing and repassing with their smiles, their loads of cut wood, made me feel both quickened and anxious, like a person in a car trying to stay abreast of a sunset.

The mountain-top Sherpa villages we camped by were always a surprise. "Where will they have hid it this time?" I wondered as, quite far behind, I plodded up through a forest towards Bedding where we were to spend the next three days acclimatizing before our attempt on Tesi Lapcha. I was convinced I was lost when I stumbled upon a few houses of a type new to me, their black padlocked stone eerily contrasting with mounds of ghostly white prayer flags. But this place of weird rites and evil mutterings (mine in the dripping mist-rain-snow of the near night) was a mere foraging center and on I trudged through gradually thinning trees. Finally at a small pass I heard a whistle. This wasn't Bedding, only the cook Passang who had kindly walked out with a thermos of sugared tea to wait for me.

I asked Passang where the village was. He pointed in the direction of some rushing water. In the gloom Bedding remained firmly invisible.

A half hour later we arrived. The faces of the children as they jumped about their brush fires in their leggings and thin shirts looked like something right off the moon: round, orange-cheeked, and very happy, as if now that we had found them everything was going to be all right again. Their teeth were chattering like children at a beach as they surrounded us, wanting to show us everything, their houses, their various jewels that they took off one by one and let us admire. Everything is always turning into night, you could hear them thinking. But it was cold and I couldn't stand around like their mothers, warming my hands in the hidden soft of my armpits.

Rather than see us disappear, they decided to accompany us to our campsite twenty minutes upriver. They were good guides, knowing exactly where all the stone crossings in the streams were, having just arranged them for their hop, skip, and jump leaps. As I walked behind, it struck me why certain people might prefer not to settle in slow-moving river valleys, among mounds of fertile clay. Playgrounds are of necessity bleak: the other side of the railroad tracks, the school dump.

There is so much that defies description, like the ghostly black-on-black of a crow passing over granite. Or the repelling crackle of laughter as the tent flap opposite lifts to a flash of creviced faces, pitch-colored, *tsampa*-licking fingers, rakish caps. The caps roof an Asiatic imperturbability as they squat waiting for the tearing guffaw that will bring them alive; yet so specific as to have the effect of a curtain being slammed down. Then the chatter resumes, words glimmering against foreheads of pine-carved intensity. Their faces are open and copper shiny, but so cracked as to seem porous, a cave to edge a finger along. With teeth of a stalactite purity from which the laugh, when it comes, will burst all jagged like an inundating sun.

□

Next morning, the village is out, so sparkly by a gray, glacial silt river as to seem for a brief moment a city rather than a mere twenty houses. These are single-story dwellings; scattered so that there is always a walled field to ensure privacy. Not that the Sherpa has much to hide. If he has a door, it is only an entrance one, shut more for reasons of wind than to keep people out. By it on a bed of straw lives the yak, great horns and fluffy coat glistening up out of the gloom. This in turn gives way to an earthen floor set off in the middle by ankle-high girders—to keep the kitchen coals in and the sleepers out.

These houses cannot be described as comfortable. Round field stones are hard to build with and the valley wind whistles in through the fittings of straw and mud. For lack of a chimney, or windows, everything is of a fire-begrimed black; but perfectly at one with yak, goat, rock, and crow.

Gradually as you walk about other notes emerge: the pied markings of the hopping, round-horned sheep; the Tang pot of a stream with its red or orange-tipped bracken; the maroon of women's dresses dining on potatoes in the middle of a sub-zero field. Across this black spectrum, to a purposeful ricochet of plinking stones, float the cloud-like shapes of a pair of yaks.

Above the village, behind a screen of pines, is the *gompa* or temple. Like churches of old the gompa is a seat of joyful noise. How much loudness does religion demand? In ringing notes comes back *om mani padme hum*, which means not "the jewel in the lotus" so much as the rolling reiteration of as deep a flowing mountain gorge as the voice can muster. Not content with the *chorten*, a hatted, buddha-eyed commemorative pile in a field, the lamas have here instituted the real article, and a fine din it makes as I stumble in to a rattling of bells and braying ten-foot-long trumpets. A stuffed, snarling tiger head guards a front door's altar beset with a birthday party's colored streamers and a miniature regatta of lit yak-butter candles. The lamas all wear watches. Their red gowns, breathing down upon their scores, emit a mist that seems to rise through their spectacles as their playing tells me I have nothing to fear: everyone is his own frog here, his own painted gargoyle. Blue knocks to white kingdoms make not only dawn, but bright laughter too.

□

In Bedding we dismiss our bare-footed porters, hiring in their stead the local villagers—virtually every able-bodied man and woman, a monk included. A tramp up to the summer pasturage of Gurung where we spend another day acclimatizing, and we are ready for our hardest day yet, over the glacial moraine to the foot of Tesi Lapcha.

Morning dawns to ladders of mist, gray snow patches, here and there a large inscribed boulder, like a heron, creating depth. The ground is recently-arrived granite. Uncollected housing? Apprentice sheep, learning how to graze? As I advance my glider-like bulk, feet seem chasms away, mouth a star. Distrustful equipoise over which I teeter, never sure when some stone won't blast out like a woodcock from under me.

As day progresses, streams loosen their ice bonds, fanning out in tiny, marble-toy transparencies. Or a pond appears, all drops of gold in a vault sliced white by the wind. In the heat mirage thousands of plovers wheel like something out of a bubble machine, a gathering of surprised, querulous voices that goes on for as long as my ink hovers and spits in the wake of a scribbled note. Then they, too, vanish, dissolved in my own glider-like tips, veers, crashings.

Twice the porters become separated from their loads. While our standard of living is solemnly retrieved we stand about, afraid even to talk for fear of launching an avalanche. Without such halts I would be left far behind, unable to perform the shifting, rock-to-rock scamper moraine requires. Not helping is my sneaker-boot combination. But my first-day blisters haven't healed and I don't dare risk reopening them a day before Tesi Lapcha.

At a glacier lake we meet a walking store in the person of a Japanese who has been climbing solo the peaks of the Tesi Lapcha glacier for the past eight days. A glance at his scarred face and one can see he has not had an easy time of it, the most recent of his falls occurring on the tricky descent into our valley. On his back is a pack that must weigh as much as he. Those with a predilection for icepicks and ropes load up. Then the brave man leaves and I find myself in tears. If getting down was so hard for him, what will the climb be like for us? We can only hope that the head Sherpa is right in saying that he must have mistaken the route.

We dine at 16,000 feet amid falling snow. Our preparations now have a moon-like artificiality: from the kerosene we must cook with to the doubled gloves in which we attempt to eat. A friend's worsening cough (her each upward step a rasp) has our doctors worried. But with only a day's supply of kerosene left we have no choice but to cross Tesi Lapcha or face an eight-day detour.

We rise next morning in the dark, so many pieces of stamping, shivering expectation. For the second time only I don these great boots, each heavy as a stair. Everything else I stuff in my duffel bag; let the porters thump around under it.

The whistle: breakfast! Tea, peanut butter, hot porridge, to which I add all the salt and sugar I can. Parkas, gloved fingers, chat above a board's plastic stools.

In prospect is a long tramp across the valley floor before the climb proper starts. With my questionable knee I want us to be off early while the snow is still firm underfoot. To my way of thinking a climb is a question of so many feet and so much daylight to complete it in. While we loiter about, bag lunches are issued, each with a chocolate bar and five sugar pills.

At a signal from the head Sherpa we finally set off, tramping across a silt of nightfallen snow. Across the valley moon-white mountains glow, the eeriness broken here by an avalanche's massive powdery rumbling, there a frozen waterfall's turquoise shimmer of dripping arrows. Occasions these to halt, let out breath to this night earth held in sky's containment where the walker is himself but mist, tomb in a valley, hope under a cloud.

At the valley end, a hill's red and tan boulders. Coughing, heads rising, shoulders pulling, we mount: hand over fist over rock over eye, in a light that seems almost solid, something I could take an axe to, carve out a silhouette—me, blue parka fitted to bright stone slab.

At the top of this boulder forest, after a slippery, axe-cut traverse, comes a somewhat steeper climb along the inner wedge of a cliff. Here the danger is less from falling than being conked by a stone dislodged by those scampering on hands and knees immediately above. The climbing itself I find exhilarating—a tree for once adult-size with no branches to threaten my eyes. Availing myself of those up to now useless appendages, my arms, I haul myself up and up. Not long before I find myself in a great bowl, alone among a group of shuffling black-and-red porter boxes.

How in their heelless boots these villagers find cliffholds I don't know, but hold they do, colorfully measuring the snow with their black-red-and-green snowshoes. Their tongues are very long and shake as they walk. Everything else is heels, heels; a walking densely pronged with earth: neck bowed, goggled eyes turned down, a great crate borne like the very calf on the back.

As each mounts, his body, spread under its burden, floats as a turtle floats in round hieroglyphic waves. You don't know whether it's his head or his eyes, but something there bulges, sways unseen. Ah, he is carrying a candle that shifts with each thrust forward of his arms, blue-weighted against his shirt. Moving, his shadow envelope stiffens, cutting like cardboard through the snowy wastes; each stab forward an act of leverage; a taking of light from around the shoulders and distributing it to the knees as they wedge along. A shuffling canal. A black weight. A star.

How strange to walk, large as a burst flower across the abalone shell moonlight. The laces on my shoes are phosphorescent spectacles as my mast-high shadow steers me forth, in white brocade following the yellowest of harps. Never have I seen air purer: jade-like glacier pits; blue icicle nails clinging to black rock. The sailing out of gloves at my sides, the stranded, fish-like gulpings for breath, all give a feeling less of terra firma than of a diamond city beneath the waves.

There has to be a catch and at the top of the next knoll it comes in the form of a blast of wind straight in the face. Rather than be torn apart, I decide to turn around and back into it. Not very fast and a bit ludicrous I can tell from those passing, but some forty minutes later here I am at some jagged outcroppings where most of our party are already assembled, munching away like gophers.

While we lunch, the Sherpa ice-cutters fan out across from us on a vast north-facing slope, orange knots of breath on the final ascent.

The wind that can turn one's efforts into all but the tiniest treadmill, can also, at this steepest juncture, veer around behind and by sheer updraft hoist me in a way I might never have managed on my own. All I have to do is to turn out my toes, let flop the parka sails of my arms, and the blast does the rest, propelling me along as one might a cart.

As if from tropic below the porters' orange parka crates zig-zag their invading lines: stopped in a huddle to gossip; or one of us sahibs sunk onto his knees as if never to rise again. But no time to dally as I plod upwards— five, seven steps at a time—the reflecting cliffs underlining this "White Ice Makes Heron Grim" that I see blazoned across my scraping, hacking chest.

Burrow my way up, how? With the claws, comes back the answer, as I press one over the other in a needle-bright pace where the wind seems the sole remaining instigator. "Won't be long now," says every smile in every fire-stained face looking down at us drooped, lordly ones sunken in the snow. I look at the angel carpet of their boots. I look at their wide-set eyes glinting in begoggled sun. "May nothing hurt them," I pray.

By now our own eyes are burning; feet feel like huge pegged posts as I struggle to shift them while wind howls and stride matches itself to shadow in the rarifying gloom. I can't see to push a foot forward, but I have to get over, here are all these fluttering red-beaked choughs piping encouragement and in a little while there on the ice-coated summit rim I am.

The electronic howl here is such that just watching our guides springing about an overhang like foxes has me in tears. But the descent ice is hard on heelless boots. Twice, rope lines must be set up. Even so, the valley is atumble with runaway crates. For me, though, the going is a dance as I stick out my arms and, legs together, hop: a woodpecker in a flight through a forest in the spring. Only perhaps not airboned enough; near the bottom I crash through, twice. On the moraine we pitch camp.

Hard time that night sleeping with the tent flaps and ropes clattering about in the gale. But it was consoling to think that, by coming upon Tesi Lapcha from the Rowaling side, we might have caught the wind devils napping. (Later, in the Japanese hotel above Khumjung I was to meet an American who had failed in four attempts to cross the pass from the Tamu side; the last, in October, by a four-foot snowfall.)

□

After the previous unevenness the two-day walk down to Tamu and along its river to our guides' home town of Khumjung seemed positively Alpine. Paths clothed me with their pines. The field walls came up no higher than my knees. Gingerly, a stream would sparkle between my sneakers, blue dwarf iris lining its bank.

While most flowers still had to await the coming monsoon the rhododendrons were in full bloom: 60-100 foot high crimsons, pinks, bridal whites. This is trekking,

I thought, as I halted by a plank; or imagined myself, a traveller in another age, being drawn across in a pulleyed basket. With no need to hurry anymore I could sit above a bank's stone-buried canoes, watching the whirl of a rapid. As their feathers circled round, I felt myself becoming this thin, scattered roar of a morning; a time spent sitting on a few rocks in one of creation's lost valleys.

Then the pattern swept by and, when I looked again, 'I' was annulled: that unencircled spot in the onswirling eddy. I could see, but I could not be; not both at once. It was this impossibility I had to understand, as if my future depended upon it. This was, in other words, no Arcadian garden, but rushing Himalayan space in all of its more acute, distressing angles asking me to open myself to the challenge of a life perpetually maintained in such a blast.

To come study in one of these cliff-hung Tamu River monasteries, how tempting, did not part of me suspect the problems of communal integration, this 'I,' 'you,' 'they,' 'us,' flailing about in vast, irregular counterdirections. However, I was able to use my knee as an excuse to forego a trek up to Everest base camp and instead spend a few days camped in a forest clearing below the celebrated Tyangboche lamasery.

With the cutting of the Tibetan trade route the lamasery had fallen on hard times. To make up for the lost revenue the lamas all had businesses: a coke-and-hotdog business; an antique business; a greasy wood-and-parchment engraving business. These in turn brought their inevitable pollution. The lamas hurled their paper cups under the trees. The Everest trekkers threw their shit flags there. Who was to pick it up?

We, of course, with our humbly-tendered baskets. In honor of its reincarnate *rimpoche* new signs were lettered and approved, then posted by the offending sites.

If I failed to participate in the clean-up, I did make the most of the lamasery forest. At 14,000 feet the eye has all these aisles to wander in, their white bark marking a quiet in which I heard my own fevers, silk-like dripping. Birds abounded, tiny rainbow fragments spun from the surrounding mist-prism. Pride of place went to the reigning national emblem, a pheasant with a peacock-blue tailpatch at the end of enormous orange-flashing wings. Almost as rare was a grouse, gray as a bobcat save around the eyes, pink within swirls of red. One late afternoon as I waded in a meadow of twisting rivulets, from the middle of a pine tree I was greeted by a loud moist silvery call: a gray flycatcher, I saw, with a long red pennant of a tail. On alighting, it revealed a cap of an unearthly skyblue set against an orange belly. There, admiring him, one rock among the many, I sat for as long as the twilight lasted, binocular fingers shivering in the mist. Greedy, greedy.

□

We had returned from Tyangboche to Khumjung when, on our next-to-last day, we decided to take in the Saturday market at Namche Bazaar two thousand feet below. In recent years Namche has received a certain fame as the assembly point for the Everest expeditions. For the highlanders of the Khumjung-Tamu region who raise only potatoes and onions and the odd yak for food, a market is essential. (How much so is shown by the willingness of traders to walk from points five and even an unbelievable ten days away.) If one didn't have time to visit the whole of a two-hundred-mile region, here was a chance, by descending a few thousand feet, to catch something of its tribal variety.

In a jiffy, a joint lit, here I am tumbling out of my tent for the climb up the ridge. A bit silly when, halfway up, I discover that I've left behind my hat. The hole being bored in my skull may be no more than a flute hole wide. But at 15,000 feet with the sun screaming like an eagle you may regret this mark that you are, traipsing along where pine trees tip green and black earth fissures away in golf-ball curves. In the distance mountains loom as always unfailingly grand, their earth of smoke silver aqua-chromed in startling blue. Excuse to squat on an outcrop, while nearby a stunted tree draws in its bristles of shade, a chough hovers in the eddying distance.

On the far side of the ridge, past the tin cans of a new airstrip, a sharp plunge has me gingerly lowering my-self, on elbows from rock to rock. Suddenly there wafts up this roar, so loud I want to burst out laughing. "There!" a companion shouts, pointing to a hillside's tin-flashing roofs. But between the glare and the ground fog I can't make out a thing. Giggling, shaking my head, I hur-ry on, wondering what compels me to behold these rings within voices within stars, this crashing cataract of match-quick humanity articulated over a canyon marketplace.

A few more hops of the rock trail and Namche bursts from under the fog: first, the crater-pit town, its triple-rowed L of houses lifted alive by lines of spanning white flags and a tall brooding pine tree. To the left, on a second hill, is the market: pinks and reds of women's sweaters firecrackling against earth and skirt blacks like so many Seurat disks.

I am trying to note these impressions, when I hear what seems to be my name being hailed. Easy thing to spot on a hillside, this Robin, and for a moment I demur, reluctant to leave my perch for a commercial circus. But rather than stay writing, "red within red within red makes gold," I decide to scramble on down, past the *chang* houses and mud lanes lined with Tibetan antique traders—each presiding over his own miniature city of relics—and on to the buzz of voices of the market hill.

Getting up on the cordoned-off marketplace presents something of a problem. I pass the one gateway where everyone is scampering up on all fours with a guffaw. It's only after I have made a complete round that I realize that I have no choice but to get down, too.

Can five hundred angels dance on the head of a pin? If Nepalese, they probably can. A more Himalayan market would be hard to imagine, I think, as a human conveyor belt sweeps me along a row of squatting Sherpas, with pitted, butter-glistening faces and hair braided like American Indians. Everything here is negotiable and to the impersonal displays of cereals, *kukri* daggers, and carpeted bric-a-brac must be added all that jangles from neck, belt, wrists, and ears. Long-skirted, thin-waisted, in their dress complete as crows, they wear these jewels and are them, colors that start in the earth as fire, emerge on the breast as heart.

Not long before I, too, am squatting among them with my own western treasures: high altitude goggles, boots, pack, gloves. Around me foot-shuffling gems bustle along, carrying bags, pulling at whiskers, grinning and counting, counting and grinning. How much for this elephant soldier mounted in wet silver, these red, green, and black Sherpa boots?

By now the first afternoon mists, harbingers of the coming monsoon, have begun to add to the selling urgency. Lacking adequate clothing, the peddlers need to give themselves enough time to make warmer ground by nightfall. By 3 p.m. the market itself will be nothing but blowing debris. In the lanes only the Tibetans are left, each in turn rising out of his carpeted incense as I pass, wildly necklaced, with jewel-dangling ears and maybe a powder-blue cowboy hat.

Outside the *chang* house a blue of electric fog marks the houses, peering out of their rock shells. On a knoll, brought within, I perch, wondering what the mist will snatch next. Here, high up, the valley narrowness comforts. I understand what the choughs are up to, flying from point to point of redness, rock. Mist circle into which I plunge my own wall-shrouded penis.

Back into the tavern for more *chang*. The figures cupped by the wall bench might be a gamelan orchestra. Trays before them, mostly bare. A black, fire-stained peace. The *chang* bowl is drunk, then washed, and perhaps another tries its wide, heron-incribed mist. No one talks. Sweeping hands, wind-red faces. Copper vessels shine like them high across the room. Now and then someone cups his hands in a flute-like blowing towards a double-tiered grate where tea and potatoes steam.

When I step out, the night is a house of blackness. But so transparent the quarter moon suffices to light up the line of a path stretching past farms and bare fields. Everything seems to be waiting. I feel very thin, alone, joyful.

THREE MAYS
IN THE AUXOIS

I HAD NEVER MET WITH BETTER PEOPLE than in Nepal and would have liked to have travelled more on the Indian sub-continent. But I had lost a lot of weight and my efforts, back in Katmandu, to eat only brought me to the verge of dysentery. So I used my Boston-Delhi return ticket to abandon the plane in Paris; a good country, it seemed, for putting on weight. A friend had offered me his house in the walled Burgundian village of Montarnis. There in the slowly-warming blue of a May everything budded, my work included. When not working I walked in the way Nepal had taught me to, feeling a tenderness I had never before known.

On two previous occasions I had visited Montarnis without succumbing to the enchantment. To my turn of spirit, wanting hills and sea in dazzling Mediterranean proximity, it hadn't seemed replete enough. Now after the barrenness of the Sherpa highlands I could appreciate a hilltop town surrounded in steep, mist-laden greens. Unlike most such "preserved" towns, Montarnis was quite unspoiled. There were no yellow parking lines, no souvenir shops, no hotel, and only once in a while a tourist bus to disgorge its prying hordes.

In the early seventies the renegade right wing of the Catholic Church (shawls and skirt in church, the mass in Latin) had managed to acquire the ancient convent and seminary, two vast properties at either end of the village. Despite a rash of late medieval palaces, Montarnis remained the same subsistence farming community it must have been when Julius Caesar camped there during the siege of Alesia, a victory that was to make him emperor and impose Latin as the new world language.

When I arrived in the second week of May winter had barely receded. There was always a frosty hum at my heels as I walked under the blossoms. But the very fragility between the white fires of night and each bluer and bluer day brought a burgeoning out, of self into eternity.

Uncertainties passed. In the morning there was jam. "Blue tongue from a crow," I'd shout, leaning out from my bedroom window, "light it, day!"

As if in response came this plaintive blackbird whistle corkscrewing up to announce there was blue in the sky once again, a wonderful electric blue in which the farm eaves across the street were like giant fishtails sailing.

Below, day, aboil in the chimney, stoked her pot. A thermometer wrote away for sun. The hour turned. To a cake of soap by a dish, some lettuce by a pan. I shivered so it was as if I held all my wounds in my fingers; then watched, helplessly, as I saw them taken away, swollen. "No one ever admits anything," I muttered, applying notions of local reserve to the dormant kitchen garden without. But then shouldn't everything real in life be, like frost, a battering in: bursts of paper; iron flies of sunshine welling from my head.

Outside quiet carts of wind moved down the lane. A man had a wheelbarrow by the hand, was prodding it through the barn door. Beyond his pegged coat, shaft-figured in light, a horse. Attached to its post like a spring to a door. The silences moved so they glistened: black nail from which I removed my book, let a beaten blade of sunlight tap me into quiet surprise. A wish rising from a well. An arrow of midnight, alone.

□

Golden-silver hour. In the glaze blue stockings of sky mount green hills to infinity. Martial and clear stand the rampart houses, slate roofs liquid in the red, clouding air.

In the long twilight how lovely to walk and watch the lilacs turn from gray to purple to an almost tourmaline pink; or come upon pansies proposing—what, but a night among themselves, all furs and crinolines dancing. Lobelia tumble from the walls in sky-blue waterfalls. Along the road forget-me-nots arrange themselves in clusters of chalk-blue mist—risings of ground into air, or into the nettle banks among which they shyly rustle, all the while stamping their blue feet.

Any twilit lane with its geranium hues of stone and shadow submits me to a world where color is speech, a series of points flickeringly scattered. Only in the sky can a semblance of continuity hold. A swan's curves might contain it all, from the first yellow-mauve to the last filaments of red. Before such fixity I can give myself, sitting entranced for hours before these transformations of taffeta or silk or satin, dust motes in still, shiny air.

To the French countryman, that blue-denimed creature of the vine with his pink cheeks and red smokestack nose, Plato's cave argument doesn't apply. For it is not sun, but a whole mottled panoply that lies outside his stone-bound fields. Where the Mediterranean sees a duel of light and shade, the Burgundian sees contours, a lip-nipple here, a bosomy curving there, each like a pate replete with its jellied mold.

In such a context a May sunset becomes a Rubensian flesh-forest, alive in its each pink hole and escaping vapor. Points, blazes, short-circuitings, here they all are one after another phosphorescently discharging, bells in a blond, sheep-capped meadow. Then others rise, more chimerical yet, dragons of the moon, breathing hulks and spitting fires, taffeta salons before whose mirrored blues another century once sank its head, its willings.

Might not such skies teach me to honor life for her very excesses: the sun-carrying of a throat; the dispersing of everything to a brown bush by a blue star. Back in my room, cloistered, awash, it is this I dance with: pink effulgence brightening to sheer flame; pink effulgence looping thumb and forefinger about her waist and with the barest of coughs smiling, all is so thick, so clear now where the sky is my life's lid and the blue envelope sinks in, nightlier than ever before. Time, I see, is rising, time is beauty, time is pressing it soft-shut-smooth against inviolate skin in this most percussion-wrapped of late twilights, clothed softnesses, me with a door between, a hand reaching out, a first star quieting violet electric air.

□

I was only able to remain six weeks in Montarnis before my friends arrived to occupy their house. But I returned the first day the house became vacant in September. I had no thought at the time of settling in the area. It was just that the daily changes of skies, fields, and flowers I had witnessed had made me curious as to what the round of a year might yield. Brought up in New York and obliged to attend and teach at urban universities, I had never spent longer than a vacation in the countryside. Now I could indulge, witnessing the long leaf-by-branch undressing of an autumn and a spring that began in February and would still be progressing when I returned home in June.

Much of my joy had to do with a new rural time-clock that, like a mouse, I had crept into. Each time I got off the train it was to be struck by how quiet the villages were, lost in the trees and blue smoke-mist of the surrounding valleys.

Before in my life I had known only one time zone. If the past existed, it was only as a visual frame, a pair of Greek columns giving play to the light while pointing towards the female horn of a distant range. I may have felt a need for a world where "truth was beauty, beauty truth." But when I traveled all I saw were the usual dust and fragments. Rooms may have been there, but they were barred by locks to which I, and I felt my society, had lost the key.

The time-honored round of peasant life brought a living past I could relate to. Theirs may have been a subsistence existence. But attend one of their picnics, or poke around in an attic, and one could see that they lived, by any standard I knew, very well. There was, to be sure, the problem of access. Peasants are, by the very nature of their work, a close-lipped, reserved people. But the recent depopulation of the countryside could leave room for an extra pair of hands, or even eyes, to fill. And in a village where the families all hated one another a stranger had his value as a go-between.

The aid I offered was certainly slight. During the wine harvest I might help with the picking, toiling up the slope behind my neighbor's vigorous 80-year-old father, one of the few who still possessed an alcohol permit. Now and then I would drive one of the family to the railroad station in exchange for a generous amount of potatoes, or a few bottles of wine.

For more personal company there were the other foreign-born toilers of word and colored line. To a man they were artists with a small "a"; not out to invent themselves anew, but to restore a sense of craft and the mystery of a calling. If the past is reality, why not use it as a setting, a source of costume for one's erotic illustrations; or master perspective, the art of the *veduta*, to an extent where one could make a living as a *trompe l'oeil* muralist? We shared a common admiration for the peasant: his herbal medicines; his cooking, an art no less diverse than the more celebrated *cuisine bourgeoise*; for the lengths to which he went to make sure that nothing he touched was ever wasted. In the Auxois in February and early March one prunes the cassis bushes. What does one do with the twigs—kindling? No, one scrapes off the green shoots and sells them to the pharmacist who grinds them into a fine-scented powder, useful for wrapping things in.

Anyone who has driven around France knows how varied a land it is; each twenty miles virtually a new culture. In an area like Burgundy not only is each valley different, but each village too differs, or seems to by whether it's up high or down below; by all that centuries of purposeful meditation have built up, here a fountain, there a hermit's seat or a Roman-looking wash house. The great local art—dry stone masonry—assured that wherever you walked you had something to try to appreciate.

Gradually the notion of staying on began to occur. The Auxois I found myself in wasn't Greece or Nepal. Nor was it the France I would have picked, given the opportunity. But unlike Greece or Nepal I felt at home. Each time I went for a walk I learned something: about what fits where and with what; about a countryside where no two days are ever quite alike. As the spring miracle rose, one layer of flowers over another, the more reluctant I felt to return to California.

This play of contending futures was to be given a twist by our end-of-season soccer banquet, a substantial ten-course Burgundian repast, with wine being poured as long as there was a bit of rim showing in your glass. After a round of joke-telling we danced to a violin and accordion played by two team-mates. At five I decided it was time to leave. After shaking hands with everyone personally as one must, I clambered into my car only to discover, as I backed out from the hill, that I had no brakes.

Does smashing up a rear axle bring good luck? At any rate, when I stuck my sheepish face inside there was a salvo of cheers and the captain himself agreed to drive me home.

On this particular morning when I woke it was to a sky of such an unearthly blue it was unthinkable not to grab pen and notebook and go for a walk. Only this time I proceeded out by a way new to me, up across the church square and out through the postern gate on the other side of the village.

On an early May morning a walk becomes of necessity a cultivation of warmths, these outcrops of sun-reflecting rock on one or another of which I now perched as if carved from an absolute of silver. As I bent my eyes down and peered at the valley green, my expectancy shivered its flames like wind. By comparison, life here seemed so rich, with all the hourly changing fragrances, all that old limestone and wooded hilltops cathedrally provide.

Then the thought came, why go back? To a writer a language counts, but it shouldn't mean living where you are constantly being soaked in commercial refuse. Why not come where I could absorb a sense of Old Time flowing even into this post-industrial age?

As I made my decision, I felt encouraged by seeing a way already paved by others' mistakes. If a cafe's zinc had its appeal in the Paris Twenties how much better to squat on this steep, barely cartsize path, noting a hill's descending rush of silences and sun.

As I sit watching a pair of crows harry a kite, up the path comes a herdsman to stroke the noon with his stick, his blue workshirt. How in almost a year in this 300 person village we had never met? To make up for that we stand chatting about the latest Ohio tornado until, with a sense of another piece of the village puzzle identified, we part, he to his lunch, I to whatever the valley has still to hold out.

Downwards, balancing on my toes, I walk, savoring these new snow-whites, yellows and blues among which I stop and peer and smell. Perfection is this thick waxy pistil of bee-intending sweetness, these unleafed willows in the meadow below like upside-down harps. Comes presence, goes complaint. Theme of a man mulling an imminent eviction.

Once at the valley floor I start to circle back. Under a wire fence, past a last violet, and into the great threads of a pasture sprinkled with tiny daisies and candelabra-like cowslips. Do I notice everything, am I still as a lake? For a moment, succumbing to the temptations of sun on raying lids, I slump down on the grass. Then a hyacinth calls, last of its tribe, one blue star atop a black silk column. Do I look for others? Yes, every orchestra wants new timbres. A few more feet and I am no longer stepping carefully. A carpet is to walk on.

By now I've climbed fifty yards and must calm my eyes with the farm textures, this postage stamp of white charolais cows affixed to blossoming blackthorn hedge and bright green meadow. On foot again, I mount to where a brambled wall appears to bar the way. Scramble over, or return the way I have come? As I hesitate, flash of leaf-fire from a sparrow. But instead of the expected wall I find a path's opening. In no hurry, I postpone it, preferring a three stone altar from where I can take in the rising circuit of my walk. By now the unearthly blue of the morning has receded before a haze frizzed with airplane tracks. All the same how pleasant to sit and feel my own sunlit waves among the burbles and calls of a wood.

Sitting, I feel able to turn any day into this transparency that invites me to look, to absorb. Only the texture is perhaps too French, too richly green. Eventually I may have to go where the bustle of moth and bird call is less; some cave at the top of an arid valley where "Who am I?" can be translated into something spun out of boots and rocks and sky. But for now the quickness charms, because I am open to each whistle, each mouth and hope and home. I want my hands to bear the long shattering of leaves as the landscape of blue turns to red, copper envelope, mist sun. To squat by shadowed moss while the bird distance wells with names: her nest; her mouth of tremulous glass. A layered attention, as of having, for a while, truly been.

With that I push my shadow back from the grass, step up where the rose of a gravel road looms. If Sherpas can live happily at 14,000 feet, why can't I watch a life slowly pass, a child's green dream of things—springing—into a force of shadows.

To arm myself against any further prevarication I bought a house: not in Montarnis, but in the cantonal capital of Vitteaux some fifteen miles towards Dijon down the valley road.

In mid-September I returned to Vitteaux and the large stone house I had bought. I was all alone. I remember a misty rain, herald of a winter that would start that very day. Below in my orchard thousands of apples of a dozen varieties were waiting to be picked. That night after an afternoon spent on a ladder, I saw their reds and greens over and over again whenever I closed my eyelids. I knew then that I had done right in purchasing the house.

Like any place not lived in for awhile the house required work and modernisation: central heating of a sort, a bathroom, kitchen, closets, shelves, as well as new roofs and chimneys. Fortunately Vitteaux was an old artisanal center. In the street outside the Lycee children could be heard rehearsing the classic power games, "Fetch me this, run!" eyes as bright with the fascinations of cement and power drills as mine had once been with bat and racquet.

To speed the repairs I engaged a trio of fourteen-year-olds who pretended to be experienced workers and certainly knew more than I about the waywardness of old stone. I got my companion to send for her brother, a carpenter. Little by little, within the limitations of my wallet, the house began to come alive. A landscape of cement waves—or was it mountains—appeared in the skirting of the W.C. Marijuana seeds, brought back from Nepal, sprouted in the conservatory, giving bluish-green plants as tall as a hollyhock. I bought a cafe's soccer game for the conservatory, and a pair of ewes with their lambs to mow the park; so successfully that the old piano teacher across the street asked if she could contribute her own menagerie—a pair of nanny goats, a blind goose, three ducks and a hen—and promptly took up a well-earned retirement at the local hospital.

For these first years the novelty of my house and what I was learning was more than enough to sustain me. Yet I could see that the rural consciousness I sought would be slow in coming. You can work alongside a peasant, grow most of your food, and in your dress and style of life, generally imitate him. Yet to acquire the essential clock, of what and when to plant, you almost have to be born into a farm home. Meanwhile the work in restoring my house was giving me a sense of other realities besides those of nature. At what point, and muttering what apologies, would the traveller re-enter the human museum?

It must be said that the dwindling valley crossroads town I found myself in did not encourage any life commitment. In the twenty-five years since the end of the war Vitteaux had lost two-thirds of its population. And, despite the power wielded by a deputy-mayor of the reigning party, it would decline by another five hundred to a thousand during my own sojourn. This couldn't help but affect me. When people stretched forth a hand to invite me into their homes all I felt was a certain feverishness, as if only I were alive.

Most of them had come to Vitteaux for the same reason as I—because houses were cheap, and with the savings one could start a small business. But there are reasons why houses are cheap and sometimes walking about their gray stone facades under a Poussin-blue winter evening sky I could imagine myself in some forlorn Greek hill village. However beautiful the views, the odd old bridge and tower and grand house, there was something definitely ghostly that made me question my own motives for continuing to live here. I could see that at forty a house might occupy the role of a lover, or a job, years earlier. But this should not mean burying myself in a backwater where I was likely to remain an outsider. For all the aggravation my fundamental life was concerned, not with rural France, but America.

In such circumstances one might see me of a May morning writing, "The metaphor of flying is acute." If "flying" is so acute, what of "dying;" or, to squeeze the rhyme once again, "lying?" At that, I feel a surge of red, red vibrations filling my skull with pulsing headache clarity; while beneath, as on an egg, sits this man, sunshaven, typing. In a poem "flying" might be an Icarus released. At the moment, however, it tacks me down with a reminder of all closing me in, this one elongating frame of a life. Can't I get up, button on a shirt, and go? But what of my animals, all those various time clocks forever going off in the fields?

Once again I can feel travel's gaudy rims descending about my nose. But hooked to my comfort I sit, feeling my window can make a house more still. Outside the countryside is blue by hillside greens and red-roofed village stone. Time to walk out, open the door of a day.

To a dream of shoes in wind feet stir, down past the rampart grotto to where an old stone bench mutes my park's unfinished order. Below, apple trees blossom, a few still so white. Grasses float high—to knee, waist. And branches sway down their shifting myopic peace. An unfinished collection is the world, a delicate house in the sun

thousands of stones old: the walled stillness forever
breaking like rain out of fog, tempering my mist with the
sense of something quiet growing—snails among blue
bottles of periwinkle vines.

Change place, light my cigarette with this new
birth of sailing cloud, this rose order that so unstills as to
make the branches seem features in a now more general
melody? Overhead, a pine cone forms rich rust, rust-
velvet ascensions, like a peasant's corduroy jacket. The
ground is stuffed with struggling density, "I'm the tall-
est," "No, you are," a whole argument in flower and
grass and nettle. How full the wet stirrings of faith, how
close to everything I must lace myself—was the reed that
way? In the long emerald floating stillness, among blackbird and river, I sit, a stocking filling against winter. The
stone step under me is dry. I will not go away. Cavaliers
and rustic orphans are here, sings the bush in the wood,
spots of lilac amid sun.

How is the wind doing—go see? Temptation be-
ing a boat, I rise, letting the hollows of a hazelnut alley
pull me where my eye touches plentiful distance, the hope
and charm of sheep, hens and roosters, planted things.
Across a property wall a reaching tong of voices blends
with the river smoke and steam. I am in a painting. Casual
sunlight brings dew lace.

Beyond a fir wood's call of buried treasure, charolais cows blossom among orchard gold like still cigarettes.
Afternoon waves a diaper cloud. I am a boat in a meadow
picking nylon strings. Somewhere out of sight a settling
crow sinks its claws into the orchard ground. I, too, have
escaped, buried the morning within my hands.

Risen through the pasture onto a plateau behind
the town church, I let the husks of moon, of dusk, light
my way. What can be better than to live with lilacs for
friends and the odd thrush to let me know this is his, un-
compromisingly, this last station where I've once more

stopped to take reports. Slowly, moon folds me in its gravestone while, further off, hills beckon with another day's tumbling, maybe even greener slips of air. I liberate myself from silences. As I step I am.

Blue darkness mounds white light. I shelter the ram of my name.

THE TEXT OF *AND OTHER VOYAGES* WAS SET DIRECTLY
FROM COMPUTER DISCS IN A TYPEFACE CALLED CLOISTER.
THE CHAPTER HEADINGS ARE SET IN CLOISTER OPEN FACE.
TYPOGRAPHY BY LAUREN LANGFORD, PALO ALTO, CALIFORNIA.

COVER LITHOGRAPH BY VIRGIL BURNETT

THIS BOOK WAS DESIGNED BY DOUGLAS CRUICKSHANK

PORTRAIT: RUPERT SHEPHARD

ROBIN MAGOWAN